TRANSPORTATION ISSUES, POLICIES AND R&D

AIRLINE COMPETITION AND CONSOLIDATION

ISSUES AND TRENDS

TRANSPORTATION ISSUES, POLICIES AND R&D

Additional books in this series can be found on Nova's website under the Series tab.

Additional e-books in this series can be found on Nova's website under the e-book tab.

TRANSPORTATION ISSUES, POLICIES AND R&D

AIRLINE COMPETITION AND CONSOLIDATION

ISSUES AND TRENDS

CAROLINE REID
EDITOR

nova publishers
New York

For permission to use material from this book please contact us:
Telephone 631-231-7269; Fax 631-231-8175
Web Site: http://www.novapublishers.com

Additional color graphics may be available in the e-book version of this book.

Library of Congress Cataloging-in-Publication Data

ISBN: 978-1-63463-119-8

Published by Nova Science Publishers, Inc. † New York

CONTENTS

Preface		**vii**
Chapter 1	Airline Competition: The Average Number of Competitors in Markets Serving the Majority of Passengers Has Changed Little in Recent Years, but Stakeholders Voice Concerns about Competition *United States Government Accountability Office*	**1**
Chapter 2	Airline Mergers: Issues Raised by the Proposed Merger of American Airlines and US Airways. Statement of Gerald L. Dillingham, Director, Physical Infrastructure Issues, Government Accountability Office. Hearing on "Airline Industry Consolidation"	**61**
Chapter 3	Reductions in Competition Increase Airline Flight Delays and Cancellations *U.S. Department of Transportation, Office of Inspector General*	**87**
Index		**113**

PREFACE

Since 2007, there have been four major airline mergers. As a result of this consolidation, about 85 percent of passengers in the U.S. flew on four domestic airlines in 2013. Certain industry observers have raised concerns that consolidation could have adverse effects on airline competition, such as higher airfares and reduced service. Others argue that consumers stand to benefit from recent changes in the industry as profitable airlines reinvest in new planes and expand their networks. This book addresses changes to the financial health of the U.S. airline industry since 2007; changes to the structure of the market since 2007; how consumers have been affected by these changes; and views of stakeholders on the key challenges to airline competition and actions the federal government could take to address these challenges. This book also presents the results of analyses of the relationship between competition, measured at the individual route level, and airline service quality, also measured at the individual route level.

Chapter 1 – Since 2007, there have been four major airline mergers. As a result of this consolidation, about 85 percent of passengers in the U.S. flew on four domestic airlines in 2013. Certain industry observers have raised concerns that consolidation could have adverse effects on airline competition, such as higher airfares and reduced service. Others argue that consumers stand to benefit from recent changes in the industry as profitable airlines reinvest in new planes and expand their networks.

To assist Congress in overseeing changes in the airline industry, GAO was asked to examine the state of competition in the domestic passenger airline industry. This report addresses (1) changes to the financial health of the U.S. airline industry since 2007; (2) changes to the structure of the market since 2007; (3) how consumers have been affected by these changes; and (4) views of stakeholders on the key challenges to airline competition and actions the federal government could take to address these challenges.

GAO analyzed airline financial data reported to DOT, as well as DOT passenger itinerary data from 2007 through 2012, the latest year available. GAO interviewed DOT and DOJ officials and 26 stakeholders, selected based on prior work and their expertise in the field, from organizations in sectors such as academia, airlines, consumer advocacy, and finance. Their views are not generalizable, but provide perspectives on a range of competition issues. Both DOJ and DOT provided technical comments on a draft of this report, which were incorporated as appropriate.

Chapter 2 – In February 2013, American and US Airways announced plans to merge the two airlines and entered into a merger agreement. Valued at $11 billion, the merged airline would retain the American name and be headquartered in Dallas-Fort Worth. This follows the mergers of United Airlines and Continental Airlines in 2010 and the acquisition of Northwest Airlines by Delta Air Lines (Delta) in 2008. This latest merger, if not challenged by DOJ, would surpass these prior mergers in scope to create the largest passenger airline in the United States. The passenger airline industry has struggled financially over the last decade and these two airlines believe a merger will strengthen them. However, as with any merger of this magnitude, this proposal will be examined by DOJ to determine if its potential benefits for consumers outweigh the potential negative effects.

This testimony focuses on (1) the role of federal authorities in reviewing merger proposals, (2) key factors motivating airline mergers in recent years, and (3) the implications of merging American and US Airways. To address these objectives, GAO drew from its previous reports on the potential effects of prior airline mergers and the financial condition of the airline industry issued from July 2008 through May 2010. GAO also analyzed DOT's airline operating and financial data, airline financial documents, and airline schedule information since 2002.

Chapter 3 – Since 2005, the U.S. airline industry's service quality—airlines' on-time performance and cancellation rates—has varied greatly. Considerable industry consolidation has also occurred since 2005, with three mergers involving six major carriers.

This report presents the results of analyses of the relationship between competition, measured at the individual route level, and airline service quality, also measured at the individual route level. The objective was to determine whether limited competition affects flight delays and cancellations. These determinations included whether (1) reductions in competition affected the percentage of late flights and the length of flight delays, (2) reductions in competition affected flight cancellation rates, and (3) the effects of reduced competition on airline service quality depended upon the initial level of competition.

In: Airline Competition and Consolidation ISBN: 978-1-63463-119-8
Editor: Caroline Reid

Chapter 1

AIRLINE COMPETITION: THE AVERAGE NUMBER OF COMPETITORS IN MARKETS SERVING THE MAJORITY OF PASSENGERS HAS CHANGED LITTLE IN RECENT YEARS, BUT STAKEHOLDERS VOICE CONCERNS ABOUT COMPETITION*

United States Government Accountability Office

WHY GAO DID THIS STUDY

Since 2007, there have been four major airline mergers. As a result of this consolidation, about 85 percent of passengers in the U.S. flew on four domestic airlines in 2013. Certain industry observers have raised concerns that consolidation could have adverse effects on airline competition, such as higher airfares and reduced service. Others argue that consumers stand to benefit from recent changes in the industry as profitable airlines reinvest in new planes and expand their networks.

To assist Congress in overseeing changes in the airline industry, GAO was asked to examine the state of competition in the domestic passenger airline industry. This report addresses (1) changes to the financial health of the U.S.

* This is an edited, reformatted and augmented version of the United States Government Accountability Office publication, GAO-14-515, dated June 2014.

airline industry since 2007; (2) changes to the structure of the market since 2007; (3) how consumers have been affected by these changes; and (4) views of stakeholders on the key challenges to airline competition and actions the federal government could take to address these challenges.

GAO analyzed airline financial data reported to DOT, as well as DOT passenger itinerary data from 2007 through 2012, the latest year available. GAO interviewed DOT and DOJ officials and 26 stakeholders, selected based on prior work and their expertise in the field, from organizations in sectors such as academia, airlines, consumer advocacy, and finance. Their views are not generalizable, but provide perspectives on a range of competition issues. Both DOJ and DOT provided technical comments on a draft of this report, which were incorporated as appropriate.

WHAT GAO FOUND

The U.S. passenger airline industry has returned to profitability following the recent economic recession. From 2007 through 2012, the industry generated approximately $21.7 billion in operating profits despite losing about $5.6 billion in 2008. U.S. airlines maintained approximately $13 billion in cash reserves in 2012. Growth in revenue has driven industry profits, aided by increased passenger traffic, "capacity restraint," (i.e., limiting the supply of available seats in relation to the level of demand), and revenue from ancillary fees for checking bags and other services. For example, baggage and reservation change fees collected by U.S. airlines increased from about $1.4 billion in 2007 to $6 billion in 2012. Additionally, unlike prior recoveries when airline capacity growth undermined the ability to charge profitable fares, airlines since 2009 have restrained capacity growth even though demand for air travel has risen with the economic recovery.

In recent years, the average number of competitors has not substantially changed in markets traveled by the majority of passengers, despite several major airline mergers. From 2007 through 2012, the average number of effective competitors (defined as airlines with more than a 5 percent market share) ranged from 4.3 to 4.5 in the markets with the most passengers. During this period, the average number of effective competitors in markets with the fewest passengers decreased slightly from 3.3 to 3 airlines. While these results reflect market changes that have occurred since several airlines merged, the American-US Airways merger occurred after GAO's analysis. The mergers created larger networks and new connections in some markets. Also, low-cost airlines have expanded since 2007, thereby adding new competitors into some larger markets. The structure of the market will continue to evolve as economic conditions change and the recent airline mergers are fully implemented.

In recent years, consumers have experienced higher airfares, additional fees, and fewer flights in certain markets, but also new services and expanded networks. Consumers paid about 4 percent more in real terms, on average, for air travel in 2012 than in 2007, without considering additional fees. The airline industry has reduced flights, especially to smaller airports, and consolidated service at large airports. Airlines have also invested in new aircraft and introduced new services, such as early boarding and entertainment options, in an attempt to differentiate products and increase revenue.

Most airline stakeholders cited barriers to market entry, especially restrictions on takeoff and landing slots at four U.S. airports—Washington, D.C.'s Reagan National and three New York City area airports—as a major challenge to airline competition. Barriers that make airline entry more difficult can hamper competition and enable incumbent firms to charge and maintain higher prices. In addition, access to capital and the size advantages of major airlines present a formidable challenge for any new airline. Stakeholders suggested addressing challenges to competition by increasing capacity at congested airports, enhancing fare transparency, and allowing states a greater role in consumer regulation of airlines. However, stakeholders differed regarding the role of the federal government in addressing competition challenges, in part because changes to the airline industry due to consolidation are ongoing.

ABBREVIATIONS

DOJ	Department of Justice
DOT	Department of Transportation
FAA	Federal Aviation Administration
HHI	Herfindahl-Hirschman Index
IATA	International Air Transport Association
JFK	John F. Kennedy International Airport
MIT	Massachusetts Institute of Technology
XML	Extensible Markup Language

June 11, 2014

The Honorable Amy Klobuchar
Chairman
The Honorable Mike Lee
Ranking Member
Subcommittee on Antitrust, Competition Policy and Consumer Rights
Committee on the Judiciary
United States Senate

The Honorable Rick Larsen
Ranking Member
Subcommittee on Aviation
Committee on Transportation and Infrastructure
House of Representatives

Since 2000, the U.S. passenger airline industry has faced a number of major challenges. For example, the industry struggled to recover from the economic recession that began in early 2001 and the aftermath of the events of September 11, 2001. While U.S. airlines partially rebounded from those events, record-high fuel prices, the financial crisis, and ensuing recession of 2007–2009 presented new challenges and led to heavy financial losses, particularly for network airlines—the largest segment of the industry.[1] These challenges contributed to a wave of bankruptcies and airline consolidation through several major airline mergers. Since 2007, six domestic network and two low-cost airlines have consolidated to four major airlines.[2] As a result, there are fewer major U.S. airlines today than at any time since deregulation in 1978. Furthermore, approximately 85 percent of U.S. passengers traveled on American Airlines, Delta Air Lines, Southwest Airlines, or United Airlines in 2013.[3] Some observers have raised questions about the effects consolidation will have on airline competition, suggesting that consumers may ultimately face higher airfares and reduced service. Others argue that consumers can benefit from recent changes in the industry, as profitable airlines reinvest in new planes, improve the quality of on-board services available to passengers, and expand their networks.

The recent merger between American Airlines and US Airways in 2013 prompted further interest in the effects that domestic airline consolidation has had on competition and consumers. In order to assist Congress with oversight of competition policy and consumer rights, you asked us to examine the U.S.

airline industry and the impact that recent consolidation has had on consumers. Specifically, this report describes (1) how the financial health of the U.S. airline industry has changed since 2007; (2) changes to the structure of the market since 2007; (3) how consumers have been affected by changes in the financial health and market structure of the U.S. airline industry; and (4) what stakeholders believe are the key challenges to airline competition and actions the federal government could take to address these challenges.

To address these objectives, we conducted analyses using airline industry information reported to the Department of Transportation (DOT), reviewed government and academic studies, and conducted interviews with knowledgeable individuals. Specifically, to evaluate changes to the financial health of the domestic airline industry, we analyzed airline financial data reported to DOT by airlines from 2007 through 2012 as these were the most recent and complete annual data. We also reviewed financial studies and conducted interviews with airline representatives, industry trade associations, industry analysts, and other industry stakeholders. To evaluate changes in the market structure of the airline industry, we analyzed data from DOT's Origin and Destination Survey from 2007 through 2012, which include fare and itinerary information on every 10th airline ticket sold; reviewed academic studies assessing competition; and interviewed DOT officials, airline representatives, and aviation industry stakeholders. This analysis focused on domestic city-pair markets, which are typically viewed as the basic, relevant market for airline travel in the U.S. A city-pair market represents air transportation between two cities. To determine how consumers have been affected by changes to the airline industry, we assessed DOT data from 2007 through 2012 on service levels to large-, medium-, and small-hub airports, and nonhub airports,[4] reviewed academic studies, and conducted interviews with academic and research experts, airline representatives, DOT and Department of Justice (DOJ) officials, and representatives from travel and consumer advocacy organizations. To assess the reliability of all DOT data that we used, we reviewed the quality control procedures applied by DOT and interviewed officials responsible for collecting these data, and subsequently determined that the data were sufficiently reliable for our purposes. Finally, to identify what stakeholders believe are the key challenges to competition and what actions the federal government could take to address these challenges, we interviewed six academic and research experts and representatives from five airlines, five travel and consumer advocacy organizations, five industry analysts, four industry trade associations, and one airport authority. We identified and selected these stakeholders based on our prior work and a literature review of relevant academic research. Their views should not be used to make generalizations about the views of all industry stakeholders, but do provide a range of perspectives on issues affecting the industry. Although our report focuses on the domestic airline industry, we have included international issues raised by some stakeholders because they viewed these issues as having implications for competition in the domestic airline industry. For more details on our scope and methodology, see appendix I.

We conducted this performance audit from May 2013 through June 2014 in accordance with generally accepted government auditing standards. Those standards require that we plan and perform the audit to obtain sufficient, appropriate evidence to provide a reasonable basis for our findings and conclusions based on our audit objectives. We believe that the evidence obtained provides a reasonable basis for our findings and conclusions based on our audit objectives.

BACKGROUND

The passenger airline industry is primarily composed of network, low-cost, and regional airlines. Network airlines were in operation before the Airline Deregulation Act of 1978 and support large, complex hub-and-spoke operations with thousands of employees and hundreds of aircraft. These airlines provide service at various fare levels to a wide variety of domestic and international destinations. Although this study focuses primarily on domestic competition, network airlines also serve international destinations. By some estimates, nearly 40 percent of network airlines' revenue is from international service, so domestic service is often aligned with their international networks. Low-cost airlines generally entered the market after deregulation and tend to operate less costly point-to-point service using fewer types of aircraft. Low-cost airlines are just beginning to serve international markets, mostly in the Caribbean and Latin America. Some airlines, like Allegiant Air and Spirit Airlines, are referred to as ultra-low-cost because they provide service often to leisure destinations at discount fares, but with higher optional fees, such as for carry-on and checked baggage. Regional airlines operate smaller aircraft—turboprops or regional jets with up to 100 seats—and generally provide service to smaller communities under capacity purchase agreements with network airlines.[5] Some regional airlines are owned by a network airline, while others are independent. Regional airlines operate about half of all domestic flights and carry about 22 percent of all airline passengers.

We have previously found that the financial performance of the deregulated airline industry has been characterized by extremely volatile earnings.[6] Despite periods of strong growth and earnings, some airlines have taken advantage of Chapter 11 bankruptcy protection to reorganize and address financial commitments and/or pursued mergers during times of substantial financial distress, although in some cases airlines have entered Chapter 7 bankruptcy proceedings to cease operations.[7] Some analysts view the industry as inherently volatile due to key demand and cost characteristics that make it difficult for airlines to quickly reduce capacity in periods of declining demand. For example, airlines have high fixed costs and cannot quickly reduce either flight schedules or employment costs when demand for air travel slows—the latter due in part to commitments made within collective-bargaining agreements and other types of contracts and leases. As we have previously noted, the industry is also highly susceptible to external shocks that decrease demand, such as those caused by wars, terrorist attacks, health events such as the SARS epidemic, or fuel price volatility.

The airline industry has experienced considerable merger and acquisition activity, especially following deregulation in 1978.[8] Since 2000, economic pressures—including volatile fuel prices, the financial crisis, and ensuing economic recession of 2007–2009—sparked a wave of consolidation across the airline industry. For instance, Delta acquired Northwest in 2008, United and Continental merged in 2010, Southwest acquired AirTran in 2011, and US Airways and American Airlines agreed to merge in 2013 and received U.S. District Court approval for the merger in April 2014. Figure 1 provides a timeline of mergers and acquisitions for the four largest surviving domestic airlines—American, Delta, Southwest, and United—based on the number of passengers served. These four airlines account for approximately 85 percent of passenger traffic in the United States in 2013.

A key financial benefit that airlines consider in a merger is the potential for increased revenues generated through additional demand (generated by more seamless travel to more destinations), increased market share, and higher fares on some routes.[9] Airlines also consider cost reductions that may result from combining complementary assets, reducing or eliminating duplicative activities and operating costs, and reducing capacity when merging with or acquiring another airline. For example, the combined airlines may be able to reduce or eliminate duplicative service, labor, and operations costs or achieve operational efficiencies by integrating computer systems and similar airline fleets.[10]

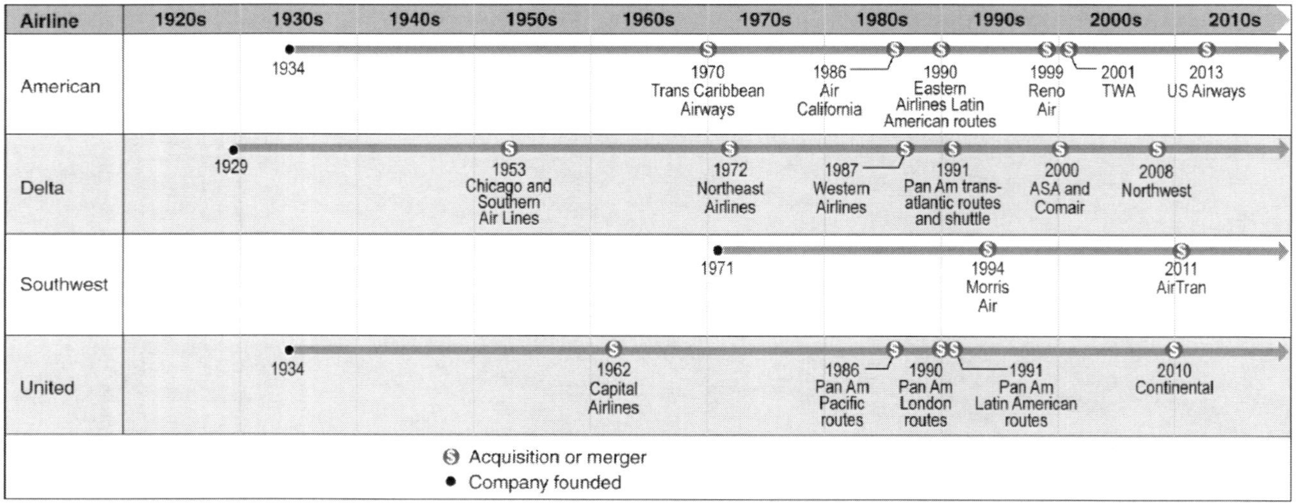

Source: Cathay Financial and airline company documents.

Figure 1. Selected U.S. Airline Mergers and Acquisitions, 1929–2013.

The most recent wave of consolidation has raised new questions about the state of competition in the industry. Economic theory suggests that competition is strongest when there are many firms in a market, and no firm has a substantial share of that market. By contrast, competition may be weaker when there are only a small number of firms because they may be able to exercise market power—in general terms, the ability to raise and maintain prices above those that would be set in a competitive market. However, if new firms are able to readily enter the market and effectively compete, they may mitigate the potential anti-competitive effects of a small number of incumbent firms, thus reducing the incumbent firms' market power. The intensity of competition in a market is not solely driven by the number of firms or the ease of entry, however. In some cases, competition can be robust in a market with only a few firms even when entry is difficult.

Although recent mergers have reduced the total number of domestic airlines, consumers are less directly affected by changes at the national level than at the individual route level. Consumers purchase seats for air transportation from one city to another. As such, they are likely to be more concerned about the number of airlines serving any specific route. Thus, a "city-pair," or traffic between two cities, is typically viewed as the basic relevant market for airline travel, including by DOJ, the agency charged with reviewing U.S. airline mergers. The relevant market in a competitive analysis is one in which the good sold by a set of firms is seen by consumers as having some degree of substitutability, such that if one firm were to raise its prices, some consumers would see the good available from other firms as a reasonable substitute and would choose to buy the good from those other firms. If a person wants to travel from Seattle to Detroit, for example, a ticket from Seattle-Tacoma International Airport to Washington Dulles International Airport would not be a substitute. When there is more than one airport in a metropolitan area for a consumer to choose from, however, the relevant market analysis could focus on an "airport-pair," instead of a city pair. For example, there are two major airports in the Washington metropolitan area—Washington Dulles International Airport and Ronald Reagan Washington National Airport—and a third nearby airport in Baltimore. Some travelers planning to fly from Seattle to Washington, D.C. could view a ticket to Baltimore/Washington Thurgood Marshall International Airport as a reasonable substitute for a ticket to Ronald Reagan Washington National Airport. In addition, travel can occur through nonstop flights and connecting hubs. While some travelers (mostly business travelers) may be willing to pay more for the convenience of nonstop flights and would view connecting flights as a poor substitute, others might weigh the potential extra cost of nonstop flights more heavily and choose a less expensive connecting option.

A starting point for any assessment of competition in an industry is an evaluation of market structure characteristics, including market concentration and the number of effective competitors.[11] These are relevant indicators of the potential degree of competition because, in the absence of new entry, having fewer competitors may lead to adverse competitive effects such as higher prices and reduced consumer choices.[12] We have previously examined a number of these market structure characteristics, including:

- the average number of effective competitors in different segments of the market;
- the types of airlines, including the presence of network and low-cost airlines, in the market;
- airline market share of passengers at the route and airport level; and
- barriers to entry, including practices or conditions that may impede a
- firm's ability to enter a market.[13]

A full competitive market analysis of the domestic airline industry—which we do not undertake in this report—would include a review of factors beyond solely market structure, including the likelihood that airlines would coordinate their behavior in terms of marketing or pricing, as well as the ease of entry that could negate market power. Additionally, in the case of a merger analysis, possible benefits related to the merger, such as enhanced innovation and economic efficiencies, would also be considered.

Both DOJ and DOT play a role in reviewing airline mergers and acquisitions. DOJ principally uses the analytical framework established in the Horizontal Merger Guidelines[14] to analyze whether a proposed merger or acquisition involving actual or potential competitors raises antitrust concerns—in other words, whether the proposal will likely create, enhance, or entrench market power or facilitate its exercise.[15] As part of its analysis, DOJ uses the Herfindahl-Hirschman Index (HHI) to assess whether a merger is likely to significantly increase concentration and raise anti-competitive concerns in the markets (principally, city-pairs) in which airlines operate.[16] Within the context of its air-carrier certification responsibilities, DOT also conducts analyses of the merits of any airline merger and acquisition[17] and submits its views and relevant information in its possession to DOJ. DOT also provides some essential data—for example, the airlines' routes and passenger traffic—that DOJ uses in its review.

INCREASED REVENUES AND REDUCED COSTS HAVE STRENGTHENED THE FINANCIAL HEALTH OF THE U.S. AIRLINE INDUSTRY

The U.S. Airline Industry's Profitability Has Improved since 2009

Sustained airline profits since 2009 have bolstered the financial health of the U.S. passenger airline industry. Our analysis of the latest available financial data reported by airlines to DOT showed that the industry generated operating profits of approximately $21.7 billion from 2007 through 2012.[18] Although the financial performance of individual airlines differed, network airlines as a whole generated operating profits of approximately $12 billion from 2007 through 2012, while low-cost airlines and regional airlines generated profits of approximately $6.1 billion and $3.6 billion respectively over the same period. This recovery follows operating losses of $5.6 billion for the U.S. passenger airline industry as a whole in 2008, due largely to the economic recession and volatility in the price of fuel. Figure 2 shows operating profits and losses for U.S. passenger airlines since 2007.

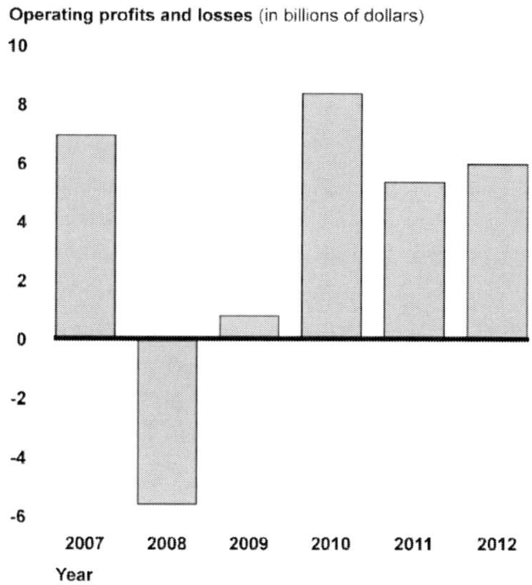

Source: GAO analysis of DOT data.

Figure 2. Operating Profits and Losses, U.S. Passenger Airline Industry, 2007–2012.

Recent efforts by certain airlines to return profits to shareholders are another indication of the industry's improved financial health since the economic recession of 2007–2009. For example, Delta Air Lines paid a quarterly dividend in 2013—its first since 2003—and plans to pay $1 billion in dividends to its shareholders over the next several years. The airline also announced a program to repurchase $500 million in shares of its stock by June 2016 and provided $506 million in profit-sharing bonuses for its employees in February 2014.[19] Industry analysts we spoke with said that other network airlines would likely follow Delta and introduce dividends in the near term. Additionally, Southwest—the only airline offering a share dividend previously—quadrupled its quarterly dividend in May 2013, increased its share buy-back program, and announced $228 million in annual profit-sharing with its employees in 2014, an increase from $121 million in 2013.

We found that improved profitability has enabled airlines to raise their liquidity in recent years by increasing their total cash reserves. Liquidity levels are especially important in the airline industry because cash balances help the airlines withstand potential industry shocks, such as lower travel demand or more volatile fuel prices, as well as pay down debt and reduce the risk of bankruptcy. U.S. airlines as a whole have increased their cash reserves from approximately $8 billion in 2007 to approximately $13 billion in 2012.

Network airlines have also generally reduced their long-term debt and certain airlines improved their credit position. Network airlines reduced long-term debt 3.7 percent (or approximately $1.2 billion) from 2007 to 2012, while low-cost airlines saw an increase in their long-term debt of 1.6 percent (or approximately $97 million) over this period. Debt reduction by network airlines has resulted in some improvement in credit profiles and credit rating upgrades for certain airlines. For example, in June 2013 Fitch Ratings Service revised its ratings outlook for Delta Air Lines from stable to positive, and in March 2014 upgraded the issuer default rating from B+ to BB-.[20] Among low-cost airlines, Southwest Airlines remains the only airline with a credit rating that is considered investment grade, which indicates relatively low to moderate credit risk. Fitch affirmed the airline's rating at BBB in September 2013. Improved credit ratings help airlines lower the cost of capital by enabling them to obtain financing—including the refinancing of existing debt—at more advantageous terms. Credit rating analysts we spoke to emphasized, however, that the industry remains significantly leveraged with debt, which may negatively affect their credit ratings.

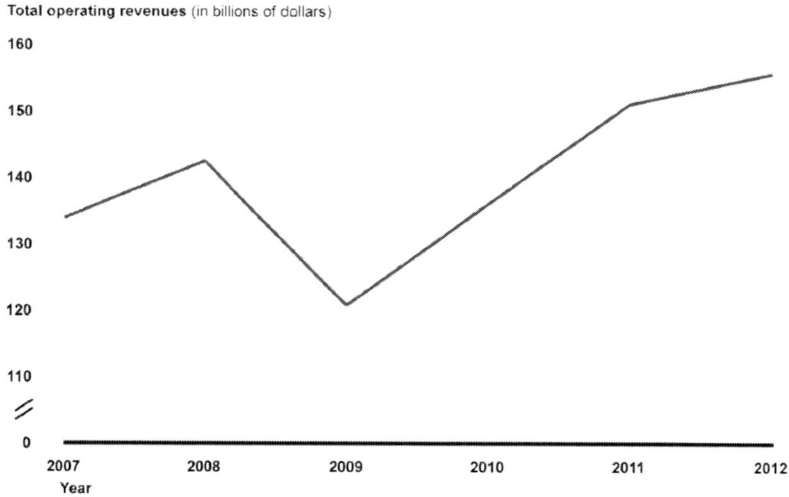

Source: GAO analysis of DOT data.

Figure 3. Total Operating Revenues, U.S. Passenger Airline Industry, 2007–2012.

Increased Passenger Traffic, Capacity Restraint, and Ancillary Fees Have Improved Airline Revenues since the Economic Recession

Growth in revenues has been a key driver in the U.S. airline industry's improved financial health and profitability. This growth has been aided by three factors: (1) an increase in passenger traffic; (2) capacity restraint (i.e., limiting the supply of available seats in relation to the level of demand), which has contributed to a rise in airfares; and (3) increased revenues from ancillary fees. Total operating revenues decreased by nearly $22 billion from 2008 to 2009 due largely to the recession, but have since exceeded pre-recession levels. The industry's operating revenues grew 29 percent from approximately $121 billion in 2009 to $156 billion in 2012 (see figure 3). During this period, network airline operating revenues increased 29 percent (from $92.5 billion to $120 billion), while operating revenues for low-cost airlines grew 43 percent (from $19 billion to $27 billion).

Although airlines' operating revenues have increased in recent years, net profit margins for the industry remain lower than those for most other industries. According to an industry association, for example, operating profits for nine U.S. passenger airlines in 2013 were 4.9 percent of total operating revenues, as compared to the Standard & Poor's 500 Index industry average, which was twice that percentage.

A recovery in domestic passenger traffic since 2009 has been a key factor in the growth in airline revenues and industry profitability. Total domestic airline passenger traffic, as measured by revenue passenger miles (RPMs) (e.g., one fare-paying passenger transported one mile) dropped about 8 percent from approximately 579 billion RPMs in 2007 to 532 billion RPMs in 2009 largely due to the economic recession, and recovered from 2009 through 2012 to approximately 575 billion RPMs.

Restraint in airline capacity—as measured by the supply of available seat miles—has also contributed to industry profitability since 2007 by allowing increased revenues at lower costs. Until recently, it was common in the U.S. airline market for any reduction in capacity to be quickly replaced. For example, we have previously found that although one airline may reduce capacity or leave the market, capacity has tended to return relatively quickly through new airline entry or expansion by an existing airline.[21] In fact, we found in 2008 that some U.S. airline industry recoveries stalled because airlines grew their capacity so quickly—either by adding additional flights or flying larger aircraft with more seats in an effort to gain market share—that their ability to charge profitable fares was undermined.[22] This dynamic appears to be changing in recent years, however. Several industry experts told us that network airlines responded to high fuel prices and declining demand during the economic recession, as expected, by reducing the supply of available seats. For example, network airline domestic capacity decreased nearly 10 percent from 446 billion available seat miles in 2007 to 403 billion available seat miles in 2009. However, unlike after other industry downturns, network airlines have not responded to rising demand for air travel in the last few years by increasing capacity, as available seat miles essentially remained flat (a decline of about 1 percent) from 2009 through 2012 as shown in figure 4 below.[23]

Domestic capacity has remained flat while domestic RPMs have increased since 2009, contributing to an increase in unit revenues.[24] Unit revenues rose for network and low-cost airlines from 2007 to 2008 and then fell from 2008 to 2009 largely due to the economic recession. From 2009 to 2012, unit revenues for both segments increased. Specifically, as shown in figure 5, over that 4-year period, network airlines' unit revenues increased 23 percent (from approximately $0.11 to $0.14 per available seat mile), while low-cost airline unit revenues rose approximately 27 percent (from approximately $0.10 to $0.13).[25]

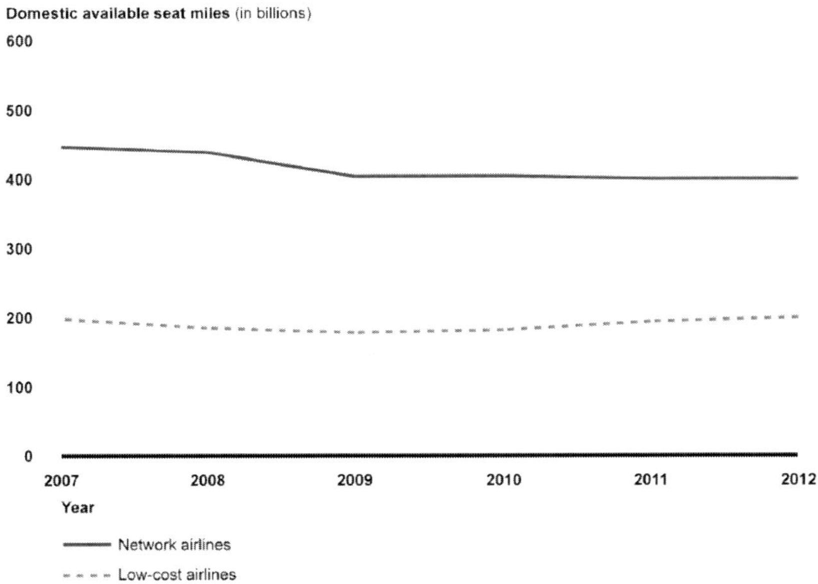

Source: GAO analysis of DOT data.

Figure 4. Domestic Available Seat Miles, Network and Low-Cost Airlines, 2007–2012.

As demand has increased, capacity restraint has resulted in higher airfares. For example, average one-way domestic fares not including taxes or other fees increased approximately 9 percent from $184.92 in 2007 to $201.00 in 2012 for network airlines, and approximately 17 percent from $117.37 to $137.00 for low-cost airlines.

Network airlines have readjusted capacity to add available seats on more profitable routes, particularly those to international destinations. In 2007, approximately 63 percent of network airlines' available seat miles were domestic and 37 percent were international. In 2012, network airlines' international available seat miles represented 42 percent of their total capacity. Network airlines are shifting their focus to international routes, in part, because they are more profitable and in these markets they face less competition from low-cost airlines, which provide predominantly domestic service. In addition, as we found in 2008, international routes provide additional passenger flow and revenue because passengers often travel through network airlines' domestic networks to reach the departure airport for their international connection.[26]

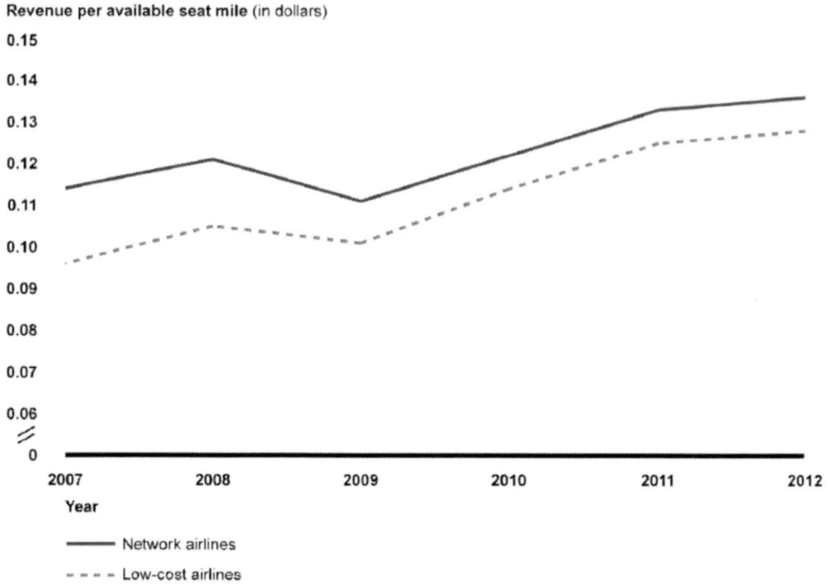

Source: GAO analysis of DOT data.

Note: Unit revenues, or revenue per available seat mile, are calculated as operating revenues excluding transport revenues divided by total available seat miles.

Figure 5. Unit Revenues, Network and Low-Cost Airlines, 2007–2012.

Airline revenues have also been supplemented by the growth in ancillary fees for optional services. These include fees for services that were previously included in the price of airfare, such as checked bags, early boarding, seat selection, and meals, and for new services that were not previously available like Wi-Fi access and other entertainment options.[27] In addition, Delta, United, and American have increased their ticket-change fees on nonrefundable tickets to as much as $200. According to industry experts, ancillary fees have been beneficial for airlines by enabling them to collect revenues that are related to the costs imposed by individual passengers, in contrast to the previous approach in which airlines spread the costs associated with these services equally across all travelers through fares, regardless of whether all passengers actually used the specific services. Ancillary fees comprise an increasing proportion of airline operating revenues, although the total amount is unclear because airlines are only required to report their checked bag and reservation change fees.[28] In 2012, the U.S. airline industry generated approximately $6 billion in checked baggage and reservation change fees, up from approximately $1.4 billion in 2007. Revenues from checked baggage and reservation change fees reported by network airlines have grown from about 1 percent of total operating revenues in 2007 to approximately 4 percent in 2012. Checked baggage and reservation change fees collected by network airlines increased from approximately $1.2 billion in 2007 to $5.1 billion in 2012. Over the same period, checked baggage and reservation change fees reported by low-cost airlines increased from approximately $183 million (about 1 percent of total operating revenues) in 2007 to approximately $892 million (about 3 percent) in 2012. Ultra low-cost airlines like Allegiant Air and Spirit Airlines that offer low fares are particularly reliant on ancillary fees. For example, revenues from checked baggage and change fees reported by Spirit Airlines grew from nearly 3 percent of total operating revenues in 2008 to almost 15 percent in 2012.

Cost Reduction Measures Have Also Contributed to Improved Financial Health for Network Airlines, While Low-Cost Airline Costs Have Risen

Efforts by network airlines to reduce costs have also been a key factor in the improved financial performance of the U.S. airline industry. We have previously found that bankruptcy restructuring during the last decade played a key role in enabling network airlines to reduce costs.[29] The bankruptcy process enabled Delta Air Lines and American Airlines to cut their costs by negotiating contract and pay concessions from their labor unions and through bankruptcy restructuring and personnel reductions. Bankruptcy restructuring also allowed some large airlines to significantly reduce their pension expenses by terminating their pension obligations and shifting claims to the Pension Benefit Guarantee Corporation.[30]

Network airlines have also accomplished cost reductions by more efficiently managing capacity. As previously mentioned, there have been four mergers and acquisitions involving major airlines since 2007, including Delta-Northwest (2008), United-Continental (2010), Southwest-AirTran (2011), and American-US Airways (2013). These mergers and acquisitions allowed the airlines to achieve efficiencies by reducing redundant capacity and eliminating inefficient operations at hub airports.[31] Prior to their merger, for example, Delta used Cincinnati as a hub for air traffic in the Midwest, while Northwest relied on Memphis as its hub in the Southeast. Through its merger with Northwest, however, Delta gained a more attractive hub for Midwestern traffic in Detroit to accompany its hub in Atlanta and subsequently downsized Cincinnati and Memphis as hubs in its network.

Low-cost airlines have not achieved the same cost reductions since 2007 that network airlines have accomplished, and instead have experienced rising unit costs. For example, fuel costs rose for both network and low-cost airlines during the recent recession, and now comprise a greater percentage of airlines' operating costs. From 2007 through 2012, for example, fuel costs grew from 31 to 38 percent of operating costs for low-cost airlines, and from 26 to 29 percent of network airline operating costs. Much of this growth for low-cost airlines can be attributed to Southwest Airlines, the largest low-cost airline. Southwest's fuel costs grew from 30 percent of operating costs in 2007 to 37 percent in 2012.[32] According to an industry analyst's report, the impact of higher fuel prices has been greater for low-cost airlines.[33] This has occurred, in part, because low-cost airlines have reduced aircraft utilization, or the average number of hours that an aircraft is in flight in a 24-hour period. For example, higher fuel prices have made off-peak flying—i.e., flights that depart in the early morning or late evening carrying fewer passengers—less attractive for low-cost airlines as these flights are less profitable, and unit costs increased as a result.

Non-fuel unit costs, measured as cost per available seat mile excluding fuel costs, have also steadily increased for low-cost airlines since 2007, while network airlines' non-fuel unit costs have only slightly increased. A 2008 academic study found that the non-fuel cost advantage (excluding fuel and transport expenses) low-cost airlines have had over network airlines narrowed from 2000 to 2006, and we found that this trend has continued to 2012, as shown in figure 6 below.[34] Non-fuel unit costs for network airlines increased about 14 percent from approximately $0.08 per available seat mile in 2007 to $0.09 in 2012, while low-cost airline non-fuel unit costs rose nearly 24 percent from approximately $0.06 to $0.08.[35] An industry analyst report attributes the increase in low-cost airlines' non-fuel unit costs to the effects of the recent recession, which, by slowing low-cost airline growth, led to increased average compensation and maintenance costs for low-cost airlines as their fleets and workforce have matured.[36] Although the gap between network and low-cost airlines' non-fuel unit costs has narrowed since 2007, some academic experts point to a structural gap in costs between network and low-cost airlines that is unlikely to reduce further, as the costs associated with the extensive networks and air-transportation service network that airlines provide are inherently greater than those for low-cost airline service.[37]

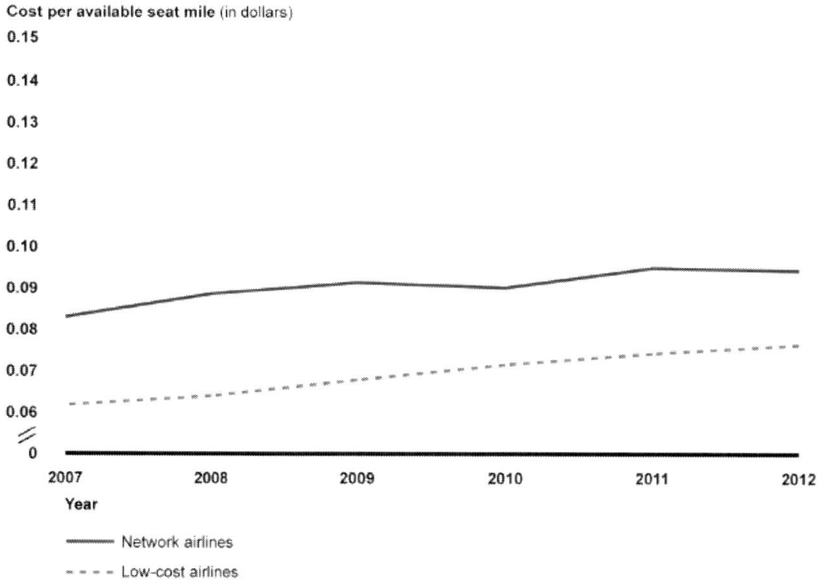

Source: GAO analysis of DOT data.

Note: Unit costs, or cost per available seat mile, are calculated as operating expenses divided by total available seat miles.

Figure 6. Unit Costs, Excluding Fuel and Transport Expenses, Network and Low-Cost Airlines, 2007–2012.

Despite Industry Consolidation, the Average Number of Competitors Has Not Substantially Changed in the Markets Traveled by the Majority of Passengers

Since 2007, there has been little change in the average number of competitors in the most heavily traveled domestic markets. In addition, the markets serving the most passengers were less concentrated than the markets serving the fewest passengers. These results do not factor in market changes from the 2013 merger between American Airlines and US Airways, but they do account for some of the market changes that may have occurred through the other three mergers that occurred from 2008 to 2011. The effect of airline mergers on the structure of individual city-pair markets may not be immediate as it can take years for merging airlines to fully integrate. Fewer competitors might have been expected in some markets as a result of the merger activity, and although we did find fewer competitors in some markets, in other markets we found that the number of competitors actually increased. The latter results may have occurred in part due to growth in network size and new connections created since the mergers. In addition, we found that since 2007, low-cost airlines have expanded into the largest passenger markets, adding new competitors in some markets where mergers may have reduced competition.

Analysis of City-Pair Market Quintiles

To perform our market structure analysis, we used DOT's Origin and Destination Survey data, which is a 10-percent quarterly sample of all airline tickets sold. We assessed approximately 91,000 U.S. markets with passenger traffic each year from 2007 through 2012; therefore, several mergers were completed during the time period covered by this analysis. We filtered the data to include only those markets with at least 520 one-way passengers or 1,040 round-trip passengers because markets with fewer passengers would be too small to ensure statistical accuracy. We also excluded markets in Alaska and Hawaii.[38] This filter removed 6 percent of the passengers from the full dataset.[39] We primarily used the city-pair market as our unit of analysis, meaning that travel between two metropolitan areas is the relevant market.[40] For each of the 6 years, we then categorized the markets into quintiles based on the total number of passengers in our sample, and for every year, traffic was segregated so that each quintile contained approximately 20 percent of the total passengers for that year. However, because the passenger traffic is not evenly distributed across all city-pair markets, the corresponding number of city-pair markets in each quintile differs substantially (see table 1).

Because certain routes carry many more passengers than others, the first quintile includes the most heavily traveled city-pair markets, while the fifth quintile includes the least-traveled city-pair markets in the sample. For instance, in 2012, about 83 million passengers—or about 20 percent of the approximately 411 million passengers in our sample—traveled in 37 city-pair markets in the first quintile. We refer to the markets in the first quintile as the largest markets. Examples include New York to Los Angeles and Washington, D.C. to Boston. Conversely, approximately 82 million passengers in the fifth quintile spread their flying across more than 9,300 markets, meaning that these city-pair markets are some of the least-traveled domestic routes. Likewise, we refer to the markets in the fifth quintile as the smallest markets. Examples include Pittsburgh, Pennsylvania to Bangor, Maine, and Spokane, Washington to Billings, Montana.

Since 2007, the Average Number of Competitors Has Changed Little in the Most Heavily Traveled Markets

We found that there has been little change in the average number of effective competitors across the markets in our analysis from 2007 through 2012.[41] For example, during this period, the average number of effective competitors each year ranged from 4.3 to 4.5 in the markets represented in the first quintile (see figure 7). The average number of effective competitors in the markets represented in the second quintile increased slightly from 3.7 in 2007 to 3.9 in 2012. On the other end of the spectrum, there has been a small decrease in the average number of effective competitors serving the smallest markets represented in the fifth quintile. Specifically, the average number of competitors fell from 3.3 to 3 between 2007 and 2012 in these small markets.[42] See appendix II for the full results of our analysis.

Table 1. Example of Number of City-Pair Markets and Passengers per Quintile, 2012

Market Segment	Number of City-Pair Markets	Number of Passengers
1st quintile	37	82,965,329
2nd quintile	99	81,452,273
3rd quintile	237	81,980,327
4th quintile	682	82,009,532
5th quintile	9,379	82,099,635
Total	**10,434**	**410,507,096**

Source: GAO analysis of DOT data.

Across all city-pair markets in our sample, we also observed a small increase in the percentage of dominated markets—in which one airline has at least 50 percent of all passenger traffic—but at the same time, a decrease in the percentage of monopoly markets, which are markets with only one provider. In 2007, approximately 72 percent of all city-pair markets were dominated markets; however, about 77 percent of all markets were dominated in 2012. Consequently, while the average city-pair market quintile may have between 3 and 4.5 effective competitors, as shown in the figure above, more than three-quarters of markets are dominated by a single airline. Although there were more dominated markets by the end of 2012, further analysis shows that the number of monopoly markets decreased from 1,712 in 2007 to 1,566 in 2012 (approximately a 9 percent decrease). Overall, we found that nearly all of the monopoly markets were the least-traveled markets, which is not surprising as markets with lower demand would be less likely to support more than one airline.[43]

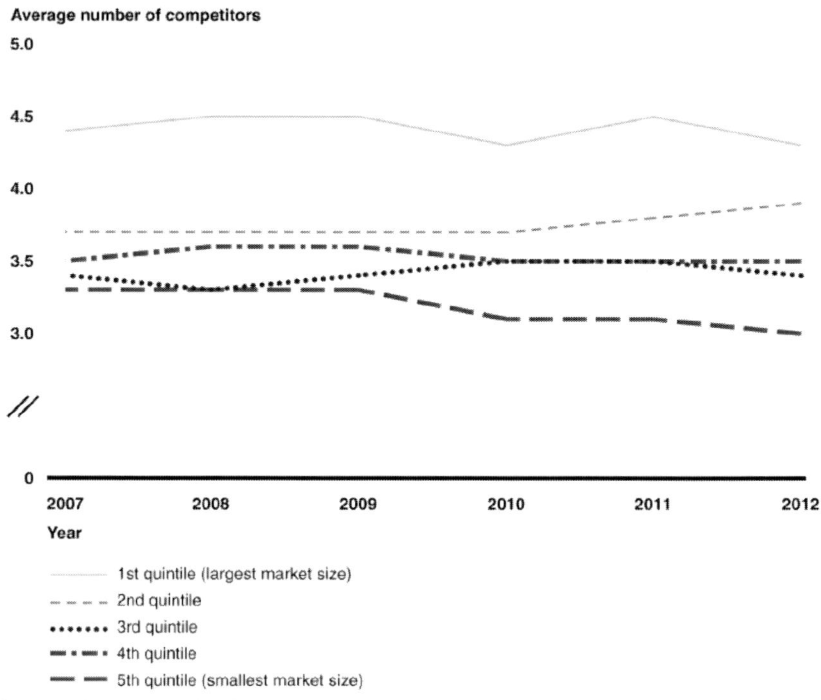

Source: GAO analysis of DOT data.

Note: Each quintile contains approximately the same number of passengers, but the number of city-pair markets differs. For example, in 2012 the first, second, third, fourth, and fifth quintile contained 37, 99, 237, 682, and 9,379 city-pair markets, respectively, each with 20 percent of the 411 million passengers in our sample.

Figure 7. Average Number of Effective Competitors in U.S. Passenger Airline Industry by City-Pair Market Size, 2007–2012.

We also calculated the Herfindahl-Hirschman Index (HHI) to measure trends in market concentration in city-pair markets. HHI is calculated by summing the squares of the individual firms' market shares, and thus gives proportionately greater weight to the larger market shares.[44] Thus, if a market is characterized by one large firm and many small firms, the HHI will capture that the market is fairly concentrated, even though there are many firms. HHI results can range from close to zero (least concentrated) to 10,000 (most concentrated).

DOJ generally classifies markets into 3 types: (1) un-concentrated markets have an HHI below 1,500; (2) moderately concentrated markets have an HHI between 1,500 and 2,500; and (3) highly concentrated markets have an HHI above 2,500.

According to DOJ, measuring market concentration through the HHI is a means to measure trends in market structure, which can provide some evidence of the extent of competition in the market, but is not an end in itself. Notably, concentration may not fully reflect the competitive significance of firms in the market, or the extent to which other factors—such as entry conditions—might also influence the extent of competition in the market.

We found that the markets serving the most passengers were less concentrated than the markets serving the fewest passengers. Moreover, there was a slight reduction in concentration in the highest-traveled markets represented in the first quintile from 2007 through 2012 (see figure 8). The notable exception to that trend is the slight increase in concentration in those markets beginning in 2011.

This corresponds to the slight decrease in effective competitors in those markets during this same time period and may represent the effect of recent airline mergers as consolidation has reduced the number of competitors overall. In the smallest passenger markets represented in the fifth quintile, market concentration as measured by the HHI has increased from 2009 through 2012.[45]

Because our analysis of effective competitors and market concentration is an average over a large number of markets, substantial changes that have occurred in some markets since 2007 may be obscured. Several examples help illuminate some of the changes in the number of competitors in certain markets:

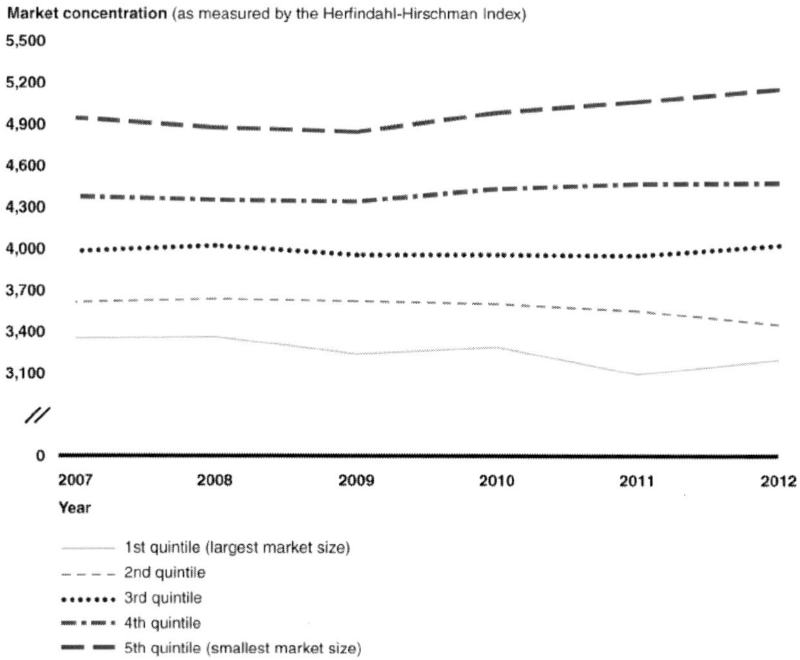

Source: GAO analysis of DOT data.

Note: Each quintile contains approximately the same number of passengers, but the number of city-pair markets differs. For example, in 2012 the first, second, third, fourth and fifth quintile contained 37, 99, 237, 682, and 9,379 city-pair markets, respectively, each with 20 percent of the 411 million passengers in our sample.

Figure 8. Market Concentration in U.S. Passenger Airline Industry by City-Pair Market Size, 2007–2012.

- **New York City (JFK) to Los Angeles (LAX):** The number of effective competitors offering direct or connecting service in this first-quintile market increased from three to five between 2007 and 2012, as new low-cost airlines entered this market. In 2007, this market was dominated by one airline, but by 2012 no airline had more than 28 percent of the total passenger traffic.
- **Salt Lake City (SLC) to Memphis (MEM):** The number of effective competitors offering direct or connecting service in this fifth-quintile market fell from six to two between 2007 and 2012,[46] in part, because of airline consolidation and changing airline business strategies, such as decisions to reduce service to former hubs. In 2007, no airline had

more than 44 percent of the market share; however, by 2012 Delta Air Lines had over 80 percent of the market, reflecting a high degree of concentration.

- **Boise, Idaho (BOI) to Bozeman, Montana (BZN):** The number of effective competitors offering direct or connecting service in this fifth-quintile market fell from three to one from 2007 to 2012.

Despite greater consolidation in the U.S. airline industry and restraint on the part of airlines in managing capacity, two factors may help explain why many markets maintained approximately the same number of effective competitors:

- **Mergers created new connections:** When two airlines merge and combine their networks, the merged airline can connect consumers to more destinations within its network than previously possible. One rationale given for the mergers between Delta Air Lines and Northwest Airlines and United Airlines and Continental Airlines was the greater scope and scale of the combined network. We found in 2010 that merging two networks expands choice by increasing the number of possible routings served by a network, as well as the number of passengers who can be served, and the ways that they can be served.[47] For example, we found in 2010 that the combination of United and Continental created a new effective competitor in 173 markets affecting 9.5 million people. For example, before the merger, United provided service to Hector International Airport in Fargo, North Dakota, and Continental provided service to Rick Husband Amarillo International Airport in Amarillo, Texas, but there was no connection between these two communities on either United or Continental. Beginning in 2012, the new United Airlines began providing connecting service via Denver International Airport.
- **Low-cost airlines have expanded into new markets:** Based on our analysis, we found that low-cost airlines expanded most rapidly into the largest passenger markets between 2007 and 2012. For example, in 2007 there was an average of 1.7 low-cost airlines in the largest passenger markets represented in the first quintile of our analysis, but by 2012 there were 2.3 low-cost airlines on average in those markets. For example, low-cost airline entry provided new competitors in the New York-to-Los Angeles market. In the smallest passenger markets,

i.e., the fifth quintile, the number of low-cost airlines has essentially remained flat between 2007 and 2012.

Additional changes to the structure of the market may occur after the three recent airline mergers are fully implemented and conditions for approving the fourth and most recent merger are fully met, as well as due to other economic circumstances. We have found that it can take some time for airlines to merge their operations, technologies, and labor forces.[48] For instance, in 2013 we found that United struggled to integrate computer and reservation systems following its merger with Continental in 2010. Also, pursuant to an agreement with the states that had joined the DOJ action to enjoin the proposed merger between American and US Airways, the new American Airlines agreed to keep seven current hubs for a period of 3 years. Those hubs include Charlotte Douglas International Airport, Chicago O'Hare International Airport, Los Angeles International Airport, Miami International Airport, John F. Kennedy International Airport, Philadelphia International Airport, and Phoenix Sky Harbor International Airport. However, the airline's business strategy could change in the future. For instance, even though in 2010 the state of Ohio and United signed a similar agreement that guaranteed hub-level service at Cleveland Hopkins International Airport, United recently announced that it would no longer be using that airport as a hub.

We also evaluated trends in the number of effective competitors and concentration in terms of the distance of the market. We found that longer-distance markets (greater than 1,000 miles) continue to have more competitors than shorter-distance markets (less than 250 miles) and that the average number of effective competitors from 2007 through 2012 has changed little in each distance category.[49] For example, we found that in 2012 there was an average of 4.1 competitors in markets longer than 1,000 miles, compared to only 3.2 in markets shorter than 250 miles. Based on the HHI, we also found that longer-distance markets are generally less concentrated than shorter-distance markets. The difference exists in large part because longer-distance markets have more viable options for connecting passengers over more hubs. For example, a passenger on a flight from Richmond, Virginia to Salt Lake City, Utah—a distance of about 2,000 miles—could not fly directly, but would have multiple connecting options, including through Hartsfield-Jackson Atlanta International, Chicago O'Hare International, and Dallas/Fort Worth International Airports. By comparison, a passenger from Seattle to Portland, Oregon—a distance of just under 300 miles—has no viable connecting options, nor would connections be as attractive to passengers in short-haul markets.

The Number of Dominated Large- and Medium-Hub Airports Has Generally Remained the Same since 2007

We also found that the number of airlines with a dominant position—carrying at least 50 percent of all domestic passenger traffic—at the largest airports in the U.S. is relatively unchanged from 2007 through 2012. For example, 13 of the 29 large-hub airports in 2012 were dominated by a single airline, up from 12 in 2007.[50] The majority of the large-hub airports were dominated by network airlines and at some of these airports, the dominant airline increased its market share. For example, Delta Air Lines increased its proportion of passenger traffic at Hartsfield-Jackson Atlanta International Airport from about 53 percent in 2007 to nearly 62 percent in 2012. However, American Airlines' dominant position at Dallas/Fort Worth International Airport declined from about 70 percent to 65 percent from 2007 through 2012 owing to multiple factors, including the entry of low-cost airlines at that airport. Low-cost airlines were dominant at two large-hub airports in 2012. For example, Southwest Airlines increased its dominant position at Chicago Midway International Airport from 74 percent of passenger traffic to 85 percent from 2007 through 2012. Airlines also increased their dominant position at medium-hub airports. In 2012, 15 of the 35 medium-hub airports were dominated by a single airline, up from 11 in 2007, and most of these airports were dominated by low-cost airlines. Nineteen of the 74 small-hub airports in 2012 were dominated by a single airline, up from 13 in 2007, and most of these airports were also dominated by low-cost airlines.

Generally, the average market share of the largest airline that operates at the nation's large-, medium-, and small-hub airports has not changed substantially since 2007. We found that since 2007, the average market share of the largest airline at the 29 large-hub domestic airports increased about 8.5 percent overall, from about 43 percent to just over 46 percent of passenger traffic. However, on average, the largest airline at the nation's 35 medium-hub airports held about 43 percent of the passenger traffic in 2007 and just over 46 percent in 2012. The average market share of the largest airline at the 74 small-hub airports grew the most from approximately 28 percent in 2007 to over 45 percent in 2012. Similarly, using the HHI measure of concentration, we found that larger airports have on average become less concentrated, while smaller airports have become on average slightly more concentrated during the same time period.[51]

Consumers Have Experienced a Rise in Fares, Additional Fees, and Fewer Flights in Certain Markets, but Benefit from New Services and Expanded Networks

Domestic Fares Have Recently Risen

As the economy has been slowly recovering from the recent recession, demand for air travel has also been recovering. As noted previously, increased demand, along with airline capacity restraint, has contributed to higher fares. We found that consumers paid approximately 4 percent more in real terms, on average, for air travel in 2012 than they did in 2007. For instance, according to DOT, in 2007, the average one-way, inflation-adjusted domestic fare was $182.72 and in 2012 was $190.10. A recent study found that average one-way, inflation-adjusted airfares increased the most at medium-hub airports, and to a lesser extent at large- and small-hub airports from 2007 through 2012.[52] Fares include only the price paid for the ticket purchase and do not include taxes or other fees, such as baggage fees. Specifically, average fares at medium-hub airports, which also experienced the greatest capacity cuts, increased nearly 12 percent, whereas they increased by 8.7 percent on average at large-hub airports and 5.7 percent at small-hub airports over the 6-year period. Fares have continued to rise since 2012. According to DOT, the average domestic airfare increased 5 percent from the third quarter of 2012 to the third quarter of 2013, the latest time period for which data were available.

Two factors likely have contributed to higher average airfares from 2007 through 2012:

- **Capacity restraint:** As discussed above, beginning in 2007, network airlines reduced domestic capacity in response to challenging economic conditions, and since 2009, available seat miles have not rebounded despite increased demand for air travel. As a result, domestic airlines have been flying fuller flights. According to well-established principles of supply and demand, a reduction in supply with constant or increasing demand will typically lead to higher prices. Medium-hub airports, which have lost the most service, have also seen the greatest airfare increases. In particular, several academic and research experts we spoke to said that airlines are now managing their growth carefully in an attempt to reduce costs and raise yields, which are the average fares paid per passenger mile. Additionally, according to several network airline representatives, airlines are prioritizing high-yield markets. That is, instead of operating at pre-recession levels throughout their networks, network airlines are allocating capacity across markets in order to maintain more capacity on the most profitable routes and limit capacity in markets that are less profitable. According to several academic and research experts we spoke with, the reduction in the number of network airlines as a result of consolidation has made it easier for the remaining airlines to maintain this strategy.

- **Low-cost airlines are exerting less pressure on fares:** While low-cost airlines continue to offer lower fares on average than network airlines,[53] recent trends suggest that the fare-reducing effect of entry by the largest low-cost airline in certain markets may be waning.[54] Typically, this phenomenon, which has been referred to as the "Southwest effect," occurs when a low-cost airline enters or is present in a market and offers lower fares than incumbent airlines, which in turn causes those incumbent competitors to respond by lowering prices in that market. These lower fares may also stimulate new demand and additional traffic. However, a recent Massachusetts Institute of Technology (MIT) study found that Southwest Airlines no longer seems to have the price disciplining effect it once had.[55] From 2007 through 2012, according to the study, fares increased the most at three airports where a significant percentage of flights were operated by Southwest, including Chicago Midway International Airport, Love Field in Dallas, and William P. Hobby Airport in Houston. Since capacity changes at these airports were relatively low, the study suggested that Southwest had demonstrated a widespread pattern of fare increases, but noted that two of the airports saw large increases in average passenger itinerary distance as Southwest expanded the types of markets served from William P. Hobby Airport and Love Field from 2007 through 2012, a change that could explain the higher fares. Nevertheless, the MIT study also noted that average fares increased 23 percent at Chicago Midway International Airport despite a negligible change in passenger itinerary distance. Moreover,

Southwest's strategy has evolved since 2007 as the airline has started to move into larger airports and business markets, thereby contributing to an increase in its costs and average fares.

Consumers Are Paying More in Ancillary Fees, but those Fees Are Not Always Fully Disclosed at Time of Purchase

Another trend affecting consumers is the widespread and increasing use of ancillary fees by airlines. As previously discussed, airlines have imposed a variety of ancillary fees on a range of optional services, such as checked and carry-on bags, meals, blankets, early boarding and seat selection. Many airlines rely on these ancillary fees as a substantial portion of their operating revenues. "Unbundling" airfares through the use of ancillary fees can be advantageous from the airlines' perspective by allowing them to better differentiate their products, boost revenue, and build passenger loyalty. Ancillary fees enable airlines to collect revenues in a manner that, in some cases, more closely matches passengers' use of airline services to the costs of providing those services. For example, providing service for checked bags is costly for airlines, but only certain customers use the service, so charging for checked bags imposes those costs only on those who choose to use the service. Ancillary fees may also be used as a means to differentiate among passengers and gain more revenues by charging for amenities that some customers may value more highly—and are more willing to pay for—than other customers, even though the cost of providing the amenity may be negligible. For example, by charging a fee to choose a more desirable seat on the aircraft, airlines are able to earn more revenue by providing an enhanced product offering to certain consumers, even though, in this case, the cost of providing the more highly valued seat is negligible.

For certain consumers, the ability to pay for particular services they desire, such as Wi-Fi or in-flight entertainment, may represent a positive development. For other consumers, however, certain ancillary fees may not seem truly optional and may increase the overall cost of flying. For example, a family of five traveling on vacation may pay in excess of $100 for checked bags that they could not carry on board in addition to the base airfare. A recent study that investigated the impact of bag fees on airfares between 2008 and 2009 found that when airlines introduced bag fees in 2008, fares fell by about 3 percent, but the total cost of travel was higher for passengers who checked bags.[56] According to our analysis of DOT data, the U.S. airline industry collected nearly $6 billion in baggage fees and reservation cancellation charges in 2012, but, as noted above, the total ancillary revenue collected from passengers is unknown as these fees are not reported separately to DOT. Moreover, consumers may not have full information about the true cost of air travel at the time they purchase their ticket. We previously found that information about ancillary fees is not fully disclosed through all ticket distribution channels used by consumers, making it difficult for them to compare the total cost of flights offered by different airlines.[57] This issue is discussed further in the next section of this report.

By Reducing Service to Medium- and Small-Hub Airports, U.S. Airlines Offer Consumers Fewer Domestic Flights

U.S. airlines, in particular network airlines, have reduced the number of flights they offer passengers in certain markets. For instance, according to our analysis of DOT data, about 1.2 million scheduled domestic flights were eliminated from 2007 through 2013 at large-, medium-, and small-hub, and nonhub airports. Scheduled departures at medium-hub airports decreased nearly 24 percent between 2007 and 2013, compared to a decrease of about 9 percent at large-hub airports and about 20 percent at small-hub airports over the same time period (see figure 9). Medium-hub airports also experienced the greatest percentage reduction in air service as measured by available seats. As we discussed previously, mergers— which have allowed airlines to reduce redundant capacity and eliminate hub airports—and capacity restraint have resulted in a reduction of flights across the country. In addition, we recently found that air service to small communities has declined since 2007 due, in part, to higher fuel costs, consolidation, and reduced demand from declining populations and as a result of some passengers opting to drive to larger markets with more attractive service (i.e. larger airports in larger cities).[58] A recent MIT study on domestic air service trends reported similar results and found that the prolonged economic downturn, high fuel prices, and capacity restraint contributed to a reduction in service.[59] The study concluded that airlines have been consolidating service at the nation's largest airports, while cutting back on service to medium- and small-hub airports.

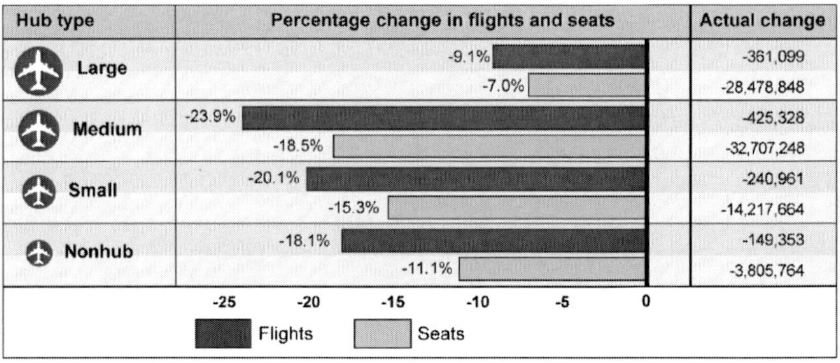

Source: GAO analysis of DOT data.

Note: Large-hub airports have at least 1 percent of all passenger boardings. Medium-hub and small-hub airports are defined as having between 0.25 and 1 percent, and 0.05 and 0.25 percent, respectively. Nonhub airports enplaned at least 10,000 passengers, but no more than 0.05 percent of all passenger boardings. The groups of large-, medium-, and small-hub and nonhub airports in this analysis are based on 2012 data.

Figure 9. Percentage Change in Number of Flights and Available Seats by Airport Category, 2007–2013.

We previously found that the percentage of flights that are canceled or diverted has been higher at airports in small rural communities than in large metropolitan areas.[60] One side effect of this trend is long travel delays. According to one academic study, the overall delay time in 2010 for passengers on canceled flights was about 5 hours.[61] This effect is further exacerbated by the increase in domestic passenger load factors from 2007 through 2012 (see figure 10 below).[62] Flight disruptions, including delays and cancellations, are costly for passengers, airlines, and the economy.[63] In recent years, roughly a quarter of all commercial flights have been delayed or canceled. Given that most flights in recent years tend to have fewer empty seats available, passengers on delayed or canceled flights often have limited opportunities to rebook on other flights, amplifying the disruptions and associated costs. These disruptions may be particularly challenging for smaller communities that have infrequent service.

Reduced service at certain airports can be attributed to several factors, including:

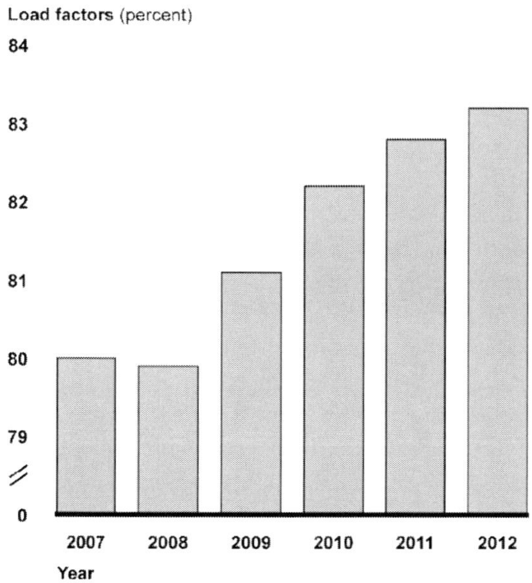

Source: GAO analysis of DOT data.

Note: "Load factor" represents the proportion of available seats that are actually occupied by passengers.

Figure 10. Passenger Load Factors, U.S. Passenger Airline Industry, 2007–2012.

- **Elimination of hubs:** Merging airlines expect to rationalize their combined networks, including hub locations, over time, in order to achieve economies of scale and reduce inefficiencies.[64] For example, in 2010 we found that the combined United and Continental Airlines would be unlikely to retain eight domestic hubs, especially given the considerable overlap between markets served by United out of Chicago and Continental out of Cleveland. On February 1, 2014, United officially announced that it was substantially reducing operations at the Cleveland Hopkins International Airport, citing lower demand at that airport. Similarly, following its merger with Northwest Airlines, Delta has substantially reduced operations through Memphis International Airport, which had been a hub for Northwest and is located near Hartsfield-Jackson Atlanta International Airport, Delta's largest hub. Airline strategies that reduce or limit service to certain airports can have consequences for the local communities. For instance, losing connectivity to major domestic and international markets may reduce the vitality of the local economy. In addition, fewer flights can make it more difficult for airports to cover the costs of their infrastructure.[65]

- **Less frequent flights and "up-gauging" aircraft:** As discussed above, in some instances, airlines have reduced the frequency of flights on certain routes that are less profitable. Instead of flying multiple daily flights to certain airports on smaller regional aircraft, airlines are flying less frequently but using larger aircraft (referred to as "up-gauging" service) and routing that traffic to large-hub airports. As shown above in figure 9, the percentage reduction in the number of flights exceeds the reduction of available seats from 2007 through 2012, particularly for smaller airports. In other instances, airlines may be eliminating flights altogether on some routes that used smaller planes. According to one airline executive we spoke with, up-gauging may be less convenient for consumers who value frequent flights, but it can be beneficial if the consumer seeks to connect through major hub airports. It can also reduce congestion, leading to fewer flight delays. Our analysis of DOT data shows that the average number of seats per flight has increased slightly for all airports in the country, with the trend of up-gauging most notable at medium- and small-hub airports (see figure 11).

Additionally, reduced service at certain airports has resulted in lost connectivity to the air transportation network for some small communities. According to an MIT study, 23 airports in small communities lost all service between 2007 and 2012.[66] The study found that network airline service at some of the smaller airports was quickly replaced by service from ultra-low cost airlines like Allegiant Air and Spirit Airlines. According to the study, for instance, after US Airways and Northwest Airlines ended service from Arnold Palmer Regional Airport in Latrobe, Pennsylvania, Spirit Airlines entered the airport to provide periodic, non-stop service primarily to leisure destinations in the Southeast.

Some Consumers May Benefit as Airlines Attempt to Offer New Services and Expanded Networks

U.S. airlines are seeking to provide greater differentiation between the products they offer by enhancing the travel experience and establishing customer loyalty to a specific airline rather than viewing the product as a commodity. Airlines are increasingly competing on service by investing in technology to enhance their websites, upgrading their fleets and airport lounges, and providing the types of services and on-board amenities that consumers may value. Network airlines are marketing their ability to offer travelers access to more global destinations through expanded networks. Network and low-cost airlines are also purchasing new airplanes as evidenced by new aircraft orders in 2013. Higher fuel prices are driving the demand for newer, more fuel-efficient aircraft, in addition to U.S. airlines' desire to replace older fleets. Passengers may benefit from these new planes because they are quieter and offer enhanced entertainment options and other in-flight amenities. Some airlines, for example, offer flat-bed seats, premium economy seats, faster Wi-Fi, and larger overhead bins. For certain passengers, some airlines are introducing premium services such as limousine pick-up at the gate. Some airlines are also waiving certain ancillary fees, such as bag fees, in an attempt to increase loyalty to their brand. Moreover, by introducing new technology, including mobile applications, airlines hope to make it easier than ever to purchase tickets from their websites. However, according to both consumer advocacy organizations we spoke with, as network and low-cost airlines compete more on service, attempt to differentiate their brands, and take steps to increase consumer loyalty, an adverse effect is that consumers have less ability to comparison shop and airlines compete less on price.

Airline Stakeholders Identified Several Challenges to Airline Competition and Proposed Limited Federal Actions to Address Them

We interviewed 26 stakeholders representing different facets of the airline industry—including academic and research experts, airline representatives, industry trade associations, industry analysts from credit rating agencies and financial services firms, an airport authority, organizations representing the travel industry, and consumer advocacy organizations—to help identify challenges to competition in the airline industry (see app. I for a complete list). Although our analysis found that since 2007 the structure of the market, with respect to the average number of effective competitors and average concentration levels, has not substantially changed in the highest-traffic city-pair markets, many stakeholders we spoke to stressed that there are competition concerns beyond the number of effective competitors and level of concentration. Stakeholders identified a number of challenges, which we categorized into four challenges to airline competition: (1) barriers that prevent airlines from entering the industry or specific markets; (2) the lack of transparency in airline fare and fee disclosure; (3) the effects of consolidation on competition; and (4) emerging international competition concerns. Certain stakeholders also suggested several actions the federal government could take that in their view would help address these challenges— including removing slot controls, which limit the number of takeoffs and landings per hour at four capacity-constrained airports; eliminating airline loyalty programs; and encouraging the completion of federal regulations that would provide consumers greater transparency in fares and fees.

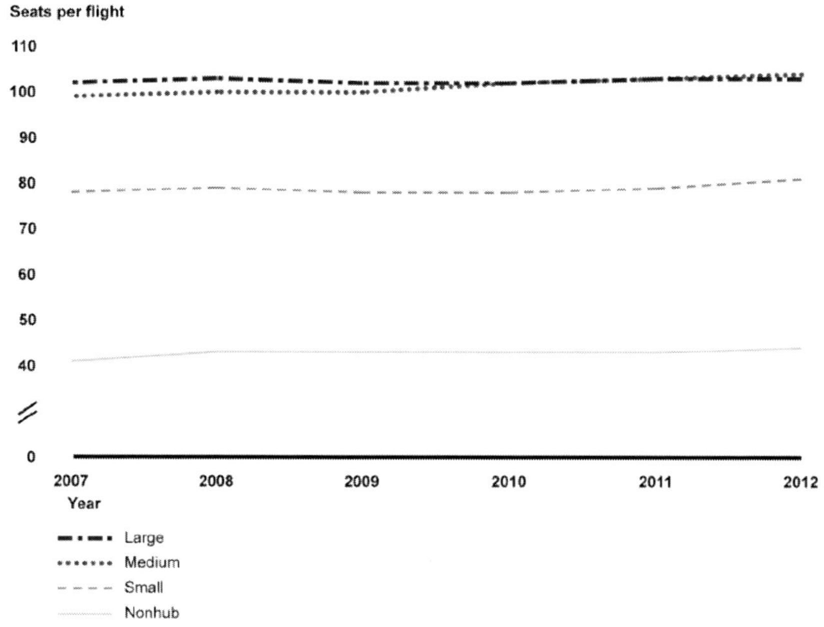

Source: GAO analysis of DOT data.

Figure 11. Average Seats per Flight by Airport Category, 2007–2012.

Most Stakeholders Cited Barriers to Entry As a Challenge

A majority of the stakeholders we interviewed cited barriers to entry as a key challenge to competition in the domestic passenger airline industry. Barriers to entry are practices or conditions that impede a firm's ability to enter either an industry or specific markets within the industry. As entry, or the threat thereof, may have a disciplining effect on incumbent firms' behavior, barriers that make entry more difficult can hamper competition and enable incumbent firms to charge higher prices without fear that doing so will attract new competitors. The last major airline to enter the U.S. market was Virgin America in 2007. We grouped the entry barriers stakeholders identified into three primary categories: barriers to airport access, diminished cost advantages and access to capital for new airlines, and advantages held by network airlines.

- **Airport access:** The inability to obtain access and secure a foothold at some key airports was identified as a major entry barrier by 10 of the 26 stakeholders we interviewed. These stakeholders drew attention to slot controls that are in place at four major congested airports.[67] We have previously found that slot controls allow airports to manage congestion; however, they also limit access for new entrants to some of the busiest airports in the country.[68] According to one industry analyst, difficulty in obtaining landing rights at these airports makes it harder for new airlines to compete for the most lucrative business travelers. As we found in September 2012, airlines that hold slots might underutilize[69] them by, for example, using smaller aircraft instead of giving the slots up, thereby reducing access by new-entrant airlines that could use the slots to offer new service or lower fares and also limiting passenger growth at these airports. In addition to slot controls, 5 stakeholders, including academic and research experts and travel and consumer advocacy organizations pointed to limited access to gates and facilities at other airports as an entry barrier. According to DOT, consolidation has made it increasingly difficult for certain airports to secure financial approvals for infrastructure projects that could allow greater access for new entrants (e.g., by building new gates). According to DOT officials, many airports are bound by majority-in-interest provisions, which in effect give the largest airlines at airports the ability to veto or delay major capital infrastructure projects.[70]

The federal government has taken steps to begin to address both slot and airport-access challenges. For example, the DOJ's settlement approving the American-US Airways merger required the merging airlines to divest slots and open up gates and other facilities to facilitate competition from low-cost airlines at seven key airports around the country.[71] Specifically, American Airlines and US Airways surrendered 104 slots at Ronald Reagan Washington National Airport that have been divested to low-cost airlines Southwest, JetBlue, and Virgin America. The airlines also divested 34 slots at New York's LaGuardia Airport to Southwest and Virgin America. The settlement is intended to mitigate any anticompetitive effects of the merger by allowing low-cost airlines to expand into new markets and provide the opportunity for more competition to the remaining major network airlines. The Federal Aviation Administration (FAA) is also developing a new rulemaking to replace the current temporary orders limiting scheduled operations at John F. Kennedy International Airport, LaGuardia Airport, and Newark Liberty International Airport and address congestion and delay issues at each of these airports. The draft notice of proposed rulemaking is currently under review at the Office of Management and Budget.[72] Additionally, DOT's Office of the Secretary of Transportation and FAA attempt to advance airline competition at larger commercial service airports through their review of airport competition plans.[73] Large- or medium-hub airports, at which one or two airlines control 50 percent or more of the passenger boardings, are required to submit competition plans to demonstrate how their leasing and financing practices will provide competitive access to airlines attempting to initiate service at those airports. DOT officials reported that the agency reviews approximately 40 airport competition plans or plan updates annually, and since 2011, seven airports became newly subject to competition plan requirements. One stakeholder we spoke with, however, highlighted concerns with the efficacy of competition plans at slot-controlled airports.

- **Diminished cost advantages and access to capital for new entrants:** Cost challenges—including limited available capital and the cost of jet fuel—were identified as significant obstacles for new airlines seeking to enter the market by eight stakeholders, including academic and research experts, industry analysts, and several airline representatives. Previously, new airlines were often able to compete with incumbents by exploiting certain cost advantages, such as lower operating costs. However, any cost advantage that a new entrant might have had relative to larger airlines has been muted by the price of fuel, which grew to approximately 30 percent of U.S. airlines' operating costs in 2012. While new entrants in the market have relied in the past on purchasing older, cheaper aircraft to establish their fleet, the rising cost of fuel has made these less fuel-efficient aircraft cost-prohibitive. Further, Boeing and Airbus have a backlog of aircraft orders, which makes it more difficult for a new airline to obtain new aircraft. Representatives from two airlines and several industry analysts told us that another factor limiting entry has been the difficulty new airlines have faced in securing the capital needed to expand their fleets since the most recent recession.

- **Network airline advantages:** Eleven stakeholders, including academic and research experts, representatives from two airlines, a consumer advocacy organization, and two travel industry organizations emphasized that the advantages the three consolidated network airlines maintain relative to smaller airlines are significant obstacles that make entry into the industry and individual new markets challenging. Specifically, according to an industry analyst and representatives from one airline, new entrants are facing a mature market with few domestic routes that are considered underserved. Further, American, Delta, and United have national networks that provide service to most domestic markets and many international destinations. A new airline that does not provide the same level of service in terms of destinations and frequency may not be able to compete with these airlines. Airline loyalty programs and corporate discounts, according to seven stakeholders, also create entry barriers. Representatives from one airline and a travel industry organization said that the corporate account agreements that network airlines create with Fortune 500 companies, which provide these companies discounts in exchange for a percentage of their corporate travel, can place smaller airlines that cannot provide such discounts at a significant disadvantage. Several stakeholders agreed and academic research supports the idea that airline loyalty programs, such as frequent flyer programs, can incentivize consumers to concentrate their flying with one airline to accumulate miles and rewards, even though other airlines' fares may be more competitively priced.[74] Six stakeholders, including representatives from a low-cost airline, academic and research experts, and an industry trade association, also drew attention to an incumbent network airline's ability to respond to entry, or the threat thereof, in a particular market by dramatically increasing capacity, thereby lowering fares and hindering a new airline's ability to profitably serve the route.

Transparency in Airline Fare and Fee Disclosure Cited As Challenges to Competition

Another key challenge cited by six stakeholders—including an academic and research expert, two consumer advocacy organizations, and three travel industry organizations—is the incomplete information about the total cost of air travel (e.g., taxes, ancillary fees, and surcharges) available to consumers at the time they purchase their ticket. These stakeholders emphasized that competition between airlines is undermined when consumers have limited ability to shop comparatively and make decisions about their air travel purchases without full fare and fee information. In 2011, DOT issued a final rule requiring that an airline's most prominently advertised airfare must be the full cost of the ticket, with government taxes, mandatory fees, and optional surcharges included.[75] DOT officials also told us that there has been an increase in complaints regarding ancillary fees since airlines first imposed fees for checked baggage. We previously found, for example, that information about ancillary fees is not fully disclosed through all ticket distribution channels (e.g., online travel agencies like Expedia.com and Travelocity), making it difficult for consumers to compare the total cost of flights offered by different airlines.[76]

We recommended in 2010 that DOT improve the disclosure of baggage fees and policies to passengers by requiring airlines to disclose fees consistently across all ticket distribution channels used by airlines.[77] In May 2014, DOT issued a notice of proposed rulemaking to, among other things, make airline pricing of ancillary fees more transparent.[78] Another rulemaking would require more detailed reporting of ancillary fees to DOT.[79] The airline industry has generally opposed this effort, arguing that expanded reporting is too complex to be economically justified and could be used to impose new taxes.

Six stakeholders we spoke with also raised concerns with the International Air Transport Association's (IATA) Resolution 787.[80] Subject to approval by DOT, Resolution 787 proposes a technical standard for the pricing and sale of airline tickets using Extensible Markup Language (XML). Airlines believe the

XML template will make it easier for airlines to offer consumers products in a "shopping basket" approach that includes the base fare as well as fees for features such as checked bags, preferred seats, in-flight Wi-Fi, and airport lounge access. However, an academic and research expert, two consumer advocates, and three travel industry organizations we spoke to raised concerns about the extent to which personal data provided by consumers will determine what travel options an airline may offer. Recently, a coalition of approximately 400 travel industry and consumer groups, including several of the stakeholders we spoke with, withdrew their objection to Resolution 787 and reached a negotiated agreement with IATA that limits Resolution 787 to a technical standard that would, if ultimately developed, be transparent and voluntary for the industry. DOT tentatively approved Resolution 787 in May 2014 and found that, subject to certain conditions, approval of IATA Resolution 787 would be in the public interest and directed interested parties to show why DOT should not approve the resolution. DOT's tentative conditions of approval include adding several safeguards to ensure that consumers shopping for air travel could not be required to disclose personal information and specifying that airlines and ticket agents would be obligated to follow their published privacy policies on the sharing and storing of personal information.[81]

Industry Stakeholders Were Divided Regarding the Effects of Industry Consolidation on Competition

Industry stakeholders were divided with regard to the effect increasing consolidation in the airline industry has had on competition, specifically in light of the merger between American Airlines and US Airways. Seven stakeholders, including several network and low-cost airlines and consumer advocacy organizations, maintain that the settlement allowing the American and US Airways merger to go forward was not in the public interest.[82] Specifically, while the settlement provides for slot or gate divestitures at seven major airports around the country, several consumer advocacy organizations maintain that the divestitures will not adequately protect against higher fares and fees and reduced service to smaller communities that may result from the merger. Two airlines—network and low-cost—also criticized the DOJ for narrowly focusing on divesting slots at several airports to low-cost airlines, while another stakeholder criticized the settlement's focus on slot divestitures without the same attention to gate availability. However, five other stakeholders, including two industry trade associations and three industry analysts, strongly supported the US Airways and American merger—along with consolidation in general—as a means to enhance the financial viability of the airlines. For example, one analyst told us that recent mergers are a market response to the financial challenges airlines experienced during the recent recession, and an industry trade association emphasized that the opportunity for airlines to combine operations has been critical to the industry's recent success.

Several Stakeholders Pointed to International Alliances and State-Sponsored Foreign Airlines As Emerging Competition Issues

Although our analysis focused on domestic airlines and markets, several stakeholders raised concerns about potential international challenges to competition. Two consumer advocacy organizations and two travel industry organizations highlighted the growth of immunized international alliances, whereby an airline may market seats on partners' flights, as a global development that has implications for domestic competition.[83] DOT has exercised its statutory authority to grant certain groups of airlines within these alliances immunity from U.S. antitrust laws affecting international transportation, thereby permitting participants, for example, to coordinate on prices, scheduling, and marketing. Grants of immunity are made by the Secretary of Transportation on a discretionary basis.[84] Several stakeholders we spoke with raised concerns that the antitrust immunity airlines in these alliances have been granted to cooperate in international markets may lead to cooperative behavior in domestic markets. For example, on trans-Atlantic routes where airlines would otherwise offer competing non-stop flights, competition may be limited and consumers adversely affected if the airlines are partners in an immunized alliance. A study by the Transportation Research Board reported that U.S. airlines that are less capable of providing international service could become weaker competitors, as they may be less likely to emerge or survive as challengers to network airlines that are part of international alliances.[85] According to DOT, since approving the first immunized alliance between Northwest and KLM in 1993, DOT's policy on airline alliances recognizes that, although the industry is among the most inherently global of all network industries, it is still subject to regulations that limit how airlines can adapt to market conditions. Unlike many other global industries, according to DOT, the airline industry cannot pursue mergers among airlines based in different countries due to strict ownership and control laws maintained by many countries around the world.[86] According to DOT, antitrust immunity is a method for allowing cooperative agreements between U.S. and foreign airlines to achieve public benefits that would otherwise not be possible. Other stakeholders focused on international competition with regard to the ability of U.S. airlines to compete with foreign airlines. Specifically, representatives from an industry trade association and representatives from a network airline told us that U.S. airlines may be at a competitive disadvantage in relation to several airlines in China and the Middle East (e.g., China Airlines, Etihad Airways, and Emirates) that they assert receive government support. Representatives from one network airline told us that by losing traffic to these airlines abroad, domestic network service could be affected as well as the financial health of the domestic airline industry. Additionally, the Future of Aviation Advisory Committee report to the Secretary of Transportation noted that U.S. airlines are facing restrictive aviation agreements in growing markets in Asia and South America and face entry barriers—such as slot restrictions, air space limitations, and local ground-handling rules—that increase their operating costs and stifle competition.[87]

Stakeholders Offered a Limited Range of Potential Federal Actions to Address Challenges, and Differed on Priorities

Stakeholders offered contrasting perspectives regarding the role of the federal government in addressing the competition challenges they identified. Actions recommended by stakeholders who supported a federal role in addressing competition challenges were in most cases directed at narrow issues within the industry, as federal action is inherently limited in a deregulated industry. Further, because the structure of the airline industry is evolving, the full competitive effects of industry consolidation are unknown.

Certain stakeholders we spoke with, including an industry analyst and airline representatives, were opposed to any federal actions to further enhance competition in the market. For example, according to representatives from one network airline, concerns about a competitive environment dominated by four large airlines do not mean that the federal government should interfere with the mechanics of the market.

Conversely, seven stakeholders were supportive of a federal role, but prioritized different actions to address concerns about competition. A majority of stakeholders did not identify any of the potential actions as the most critical for the federal government to take.

- **Reducing barriers to entry:** Several industry stakeholders drew attention to reducing barriers to entry. For example, one airport authority said that slot controls should be removed to maximize capacity and encourage competition at New York and Washington, D.C. airports. We have also recommended that FAA improve its administration of the slot control rules to enhance competition through greater transparency and airline access to slots.[88] Additionally, two stakeholders supported either eliminating airline loyalty programs or taxing their benefits as a means to increase competition among airlines. The Internal Revenue Service announced in 2002 that it does not plan to pursue a tax enforcement program regarding promotional benefits such as frequent flyer miles. As a result, employees are currently able to keep mileage earned from flights that are paid for by their employer without being taxed for the value.[89] Taxing benefits from airline reward programs, according to these stakeholders, would enhance competition by enabling airlines to compete route-to-route without regard to the extra benefit of frequent flyer miles.
- **Increasing fare transparency:** The three travel industry organizations and two consumer advocacy organizations we interviewed supported a stronger federal role in increasing transparency and competition within the industry by encouraging DOT to continue to finalize its proposed rulemaking on reporting ancillary revenue to help ensure that passengers are aware of the full cost of travel—including ancillary fees—at the time of purchasing a ticket.
- **Mitigating anticompetitive effects of consolidation:** To address any adverse effects industry consolidation has had on competition, two consumer advocacy and travel industry organizations argued that Congress should repeal a preemption provision in the Airline Deregulation Act of 1978, as amended. This provision prohibits states or their political subdivisions from enacting or enforcing any law, regulation, rule, or other provision having the force and effect of law related to the price, route, or service of an airline.[90] The consumer advocacy and travel industry organizations argued that such a repeal would allow states to sue airlines to enhance consumer protections. Since the industry was deregulated in 1978, air transportation has

been almost exclusively under federal oversight. The Airline Deregulation Act's preemption provision has been interpreted by the U.S. Supreme Court to preempt regulation of airline fare advertising under state consumer protection laws.[91] The consumer advocacy and travel industry organizations argued that lifting this preemption restriction and allowing state attorneys general to sue airlines would increase discipline and benefit consumers. Additionally, one academic and research expert and a travel industry organization we spoke with recommended that DOJ conduct post-merger analyses to determine whether mergers have delivered the benefits, including efficiencies and cost savings, airlines have promised in advance.

- **Addressing global competition challenges:** Several consumer advocacy and travel industry organizations recommended that the federal government place more scrutiny on international alliances by conducting regular reviews to evaluate the effects of antitrust immunity. Two stakeholders supported a federal role in helping U.S. airlines compete in the global market as they assert government support and minimal regulatory burdens in some foreign countries give airlines like Etihad Airways, Emirates, and Qatar Airways from Persian Gulf states a competitive advantage over U.S. airlines. One industry trade association and representatives from one network airline we spoke with were supportive of policies that would enable U.S. airlines to more effectively compete with international airlines. These stakeholders advocated ensuring that U.S. Open Skies policy—agreements that the U.S. signs with other countries to allow airlines access to international markets—contain provisions that support high labor standards and protect U.S. aviation jobs, and reject any new or increased taxes or fees on the airline industry.

AGENCY COMMENTS

We provided a draft of this report to DOJ and DOT for review and comment. Both DOJ and DOT provided technical comments that we incorporated as appropriate.

Sincerely yours,
Susan A. Fleming
Director, Physical Infrastructure Issues

Appendix I. Objectives, Scope, and Methodology

The objectives of this report were to examine (1) how the financial health of the U.S. airline industry has changed since 2007; (2) changes to the structure of the market since 2007; (3) how consumers have been affected by changes in the financial health and market structure of the U.S. airline industry; and (4) what stakeholders believe are the key challenges to airline competition and actions the federal government could take to address these challenges.

To examine changes to the financial health of the domestic airline industry since 2007, we analyzed airline financial and operational data, reviewed relevant studies, and interviewed industry experts. We divided the airline industry into network, low-cost, and regional airlines. While there is variation in the size and financial condition of the airlines within these groups, there are more similarities than differences. The eight network airlines have adopted hub-and-spoke network models, which can be more expensive to operate than point-to-point service. Low-cost airlines are typically smaller, and generally employ a less costly point-to-point service model. The eight low-cost airlines (AirTran Airways, Allegiant Air, America West Airlines,[92] Frontier Airlines, JetBlue, Southwest Airlines, Spirit Airlines, and Virgin America) had consistently lower unit costs than the eight network airlines (Alaska Airlines, American Airlines, Continental Airlines, Delta Air Lines, Hawaiian Airlines, Northwest Airlines, United Airlines and US Airways). We also included the 30 regional airlines that account for 99 percent of passengers on regional airlines in 2012. These airlines operate smaller aircraft and provide service to smaller communities. We utilized Department of Transportation (DOT) Form 41 financial and operational data submitted to DOT by U.S. passenger airlines for the years 2007 through 2012 as these were the most recent and complete annual data. All dollar figures in this report are nominal unless otherwise noted. We analyzed these data using various metrics for airline financial performance identified from our previous work. We obtained these data from Diio, a private contractor that provides online access to U.S. airline financial, operational, and passenger data with a query-based interface. To assess the reliability of these data, we reviewed the quality control procedures used by Diio and DOT, interviewed DOT officials responsible for data collection efforts, and subsequently determined that the data were sufficiently reliable for our purposes. We also reviewed government and expert data analyses, research, and studies, as well as our own previous studies. The expert research and studies, where applicable, were reviewed by a GAO economist or were corroborated with additional sources to determine that they were sufficiently reliable for our purposes. Finally, we conducted interviews with airline representatives, industry trade associations, industry analysts at credit rating agencies and financial services firms, and other industry stakeholders (see table 4 below). The analysts and experts were identified and selected based on a literature review, prior GAO work, and recommendations from within the industry. See below for a description of our method for selecting these stakeholders.

To examine how the airline industry's market structure has changed since 2007, we analyzed data from DOT's Origin and Destination Survey, which includes fare and itinerary information on every 10th airline ticket sold; reviewed academic studies assessing competition; and interviewed DOT officials, airline representatives, and aviation industry stakeholders. The data sample comprises approximately 91,000 airport-pair markets for each calendar year 2007 through 2012. We excluded tickets with international, Alaskan, or Hawaiian destinations. We eliminated Alaskan and Hawaiian destinations because cost and competitive conditions involving these destinations are likely to be considerably different than routes within the continental U.S. and therefore it was not appropriate to include these types of routes in our analysis. Since only the airline issuing the ticket is identified, regional airline traffic is counted under the network parent or partner airline. To assess the reliability of these data, we reviewed the quality control procedures used by Diio, our data provider, and DOT, interviewed DOT officials responsible for data collection efforts, and subsequently determined that the data were sufficiently reliable for our purposes. To analyze changes in the number of effective competitors and market concentration, we performed a number of steps to aggregate and filter the data. First, since the ticket data contain one-way-direction ticket information, we combined data on one-way trips traveling in either direction for a given market defined by two cities (or airports). For example, we combined the traffic going from Lehigh Valley International Airport (ABE) to Abilene Regional Airport (ABI) with traffic travelling from ABE to ABI to obtain a total passenger count of all traffic between the two airports. Second, we filtered the data to include only those airport-pair markets with at least 520 passengers in one direction or 1,040 passengers for round-trip traffic because markets with fewer passengers would be too small to ensure statistical accuracy. This filter removed 6 percent of the passengers from the full dataset.[93] Next, we defined an effective competitor as an airline with at least 5 percent of total traffic. These are the same minimum passenger and market share filters that we have previously used to assess whether an airline has sufficient presence in a market to affect competition.[94] Finally, we created separate market-level data sets based on two different market definitions: 1) airport-pair and 2) city-pair as defined by DOT.[95] The most straight-forward definition of a market is the airport-pair, or travel between two airports. However, the largest cities often contain several commercial airports that compete for passengers, and are in some cases treated as a single destination. This analysis focused on domestic city-pair markets, which represent air transportation between two cities. City-pair markets are typically viewed as the basic, relevant market for airline travel in the U.S.

For each version of the data, we calculated (1) the proportion of total passengers carried by each airline in the market; (2) the weighted and un-weighted average number of effective competitors (defined as having at least 5 percent of total passenger traffic in the market); and (3) the average Herfindahl-Hirschman Index (HHI), which is a measure of the level of concentration in a market and provides an indication of changes in the level of competition. HHI is calculated by squaring the market share of each airline competing in the market and then summing the results. For example, a market consisting of four firms—two of which have market shares of 30 percent and two of which have market shares of 20 percent—has an HHI of 2,600 ($30^2 + 30^2 + 20^2 + 20^2 = 2{,}600$). To analyze changes in the average number of effective competitors and concentration based on the size of the passenger markets, we divided markets into quintiles based on the total passengers across all markets. This means that each quintile had roughly 20 percent of the total passengers, but the number of markets in each quintile varied. These numbers also varied each year. For example, in 2012, we analyzed 10,434 city-pair markets representing about 411 million passengers (see table 2). In addition, we assessed the number of markets dominated by a single airline and the number of non-dominated markets for each quintile.

We also divided markets into quintiles based on the total number of markets to gain additional understanding of changes in the smallest markets. This means that we assigned markets into quintiles in such a way that there were equal numbers of markets in each quintile, but varying number of passengers, as shown in table 3 below.

In addition, to analyze the data by distance, we grouped the markets into five distance categories: 0-250 miles; 251-500 miles; 501-750 miles; 751-1000 miles; and 1,001 miles and over.

Table 2. Market Structure Data Based on Total Passengers by Quintiles, 2012

	Airport-Pair		City-Pair (DOT)	
	Markets	Passengers	Markets	Markets
1st quintile	97	82,394,591	37	82,965,329
2nd quintile	203	81,522,539	99	81,452,273
3rd quintile	408	81,913,364	237	81,980,327
4th quintile	1,085	81,953,082	682	82,009,532
5th quintile	11,136	81,918,396	9,379	82,099,635
Total	**12,929**	**409,701,972**	**10,434**	**410,507,096**

Source: GAO analysis of DOT data.

Table 3. Market Structure Data Based on Total Markets by Quintiles, 2012

	Airport-Pair		City–Pair (DOT)	
	Markets	Passengers	Markets	Passengers
1st quintile	2,585	353,357,035	2,086	367,070,725
2nd quintile	2,586	33,763,747	2,087	25,674,684
3rd quintile	2,586	12,703,246	2,087	9,955,800
4th quintile	2,587	6,333,036	2,088	4,975,358
5th quintile	2,585	3,544,908	2,086	2,830,529
Total	**12,929**	**409,701,972**	**10,434**	**410,507,096**

Source: GAO analysis of DOT data.

To determine changes in the structure of the market at the airport level, we analyzed DOT T-100 enplanement data for 2007 through 2012 to examine changes in passenger traffic among the airlines at each airport. The T-100 database includes traffic data (passenger and cargo) and operational data for U.S. and foreign airlines traveling to and from the United States. These data represent a 100 percent census of all traffic.

To assess the reliability of these data, we reviewed the quality control procedures used by DOT, interviewed DOT officials responsible for data collection efforts, and subsequently determined that the data were sufficiently reliable for our purposes. We also evaluated the airlines' shares of total airport passengers and calculated an airport-level HHI.

To determine how consumers have been affected by changes to the airline industry, we also assessed DOT T-100 enplanement data for 2007 through 2012 on service levels to large-, medium-, small-hub, and nonhub airports, reviewed academic studies and expert research, and conducted interviews with DOT and DOJ officials, six academic and research experts, representatives from five airlines, five travel and consumer advocacy organizations, four industry trade associations, and one airport authority (see table 4 below).

Finally, to identify what stakeholders believe are the key challenges to competition and what actions the federal government could take to address these challenges, we interviewed six academic and research experts, representatives from five airlines, five travel and consumer advocacy organizations, five industry analysts, four industry trade associations, and one airport authority.

Although the focus of our report is the domestic airline industry, we have included international issues raised by some stakeholders because they viewed these issues as having implications for competition in the domestic airline industry.

We identified and selected these stakeholders based on prior GAO work, a review of relevant academic literature, and expertise in their field. The expert research and academic studies, where applicable, were either reviewed by a GAO economist or corroborated with additional sources to determine that they were sufficiently reliable for our purposes. The views of the 26 stakeholders should not be used to make generalizations about the views of all airline competition stakeholders, but do provide a range of perspectives on issues affecting the industry. In addition, we reviewed relevant studies and documentation from these stakeholders, and prior GAO and other government reports.

Table 4. Airline Stakeholders GAO Interviewed

Federal agencies
Department of Justice
Department of Transportation
Academics and expert researchers
Peter Belobaba, Massachusetts Institute of Technology
Severin Borenstein, University of California, Berkeley
Jan Brueckner and Dan Luo, University of California, Irvine
Ken Button, George Mason University
Diana Moss, American Antitrust Institute

Vikrant Vaze, Dartmouth University
Airlines
Alaska Airlines
Delta Air Lines
Republic Airways
Southwest Airlines
Virgin America
Airport authorities
Port Authority of New York & New Jersey
Consumer advocacy and travel industry organizations
American Society of Travel Agents
Business Travel Coalition
Consumers Union
Consumer Travel Alliance
Travel Technology Association
Industry analysts from credit rating agencies and financial services firms
Bank of America Merrill Lynch
Fitch Ratings
J.P. Morgan Securities
Moody's Investor Services
Standard and Poor's Ratings Services
Industry trade associations
Air Line Pilots Association, International
Airlines for America
Airports Council International–North America
Regional Airline Association

Source: GAO.

We conducted this performance audit from May 2013 through June 2014 in accordance with generally accepted auditing standards. Those standards require that we plan and perform the audit to obtain sufficient, appropriate evidence to provide a reasonable basis for our findings and conclusions based on our audit objectives.

We believe that the evidence obtained provides a reasonable basis for our findings and conclusions based on our audit objectives.

APPENDIX II. RESULTS OF MARKET STRUCTURE ANALYSIS FOR THE U.S. PASSENGER AIRLINE INDUSTRY, 2007–2012

Table 5. Average Number of Effective Competitors by Airport-Pair Market Size

	2007	2008	2009	2010	2011	2012
1st quintile (largest market size)	2.8	2.7	2.9	2.9	3	3.1
2nd quintile	2.4	2.4	2.4	2.5	2.6	2.5
3rd quintile	2.5	2.5	2.6	2.6	2.6	2.7
4th quintile	3.1	3.2	3.2	3.1	3.1	3.1
5th quintile (smallest market size)	3.2	3.2	3.2	3	3	2.8

Source: GAO analysis of DOT data.

Table 6. Average Number of Effective Competitors by City-Pair Market Size

	2007	2008	2009	2010	2011	2012
1st quintile	4.4	4.5	4.5	4.3	4.5	4.3
2nd quintile	3.7	3.7	3.7	3.7	3.8	3.9
3rd quintile	3.4	3.3	3.4	3.5	3.5	3.4
4th quintile	3.5	3.6	3.6	3.5	3.5	3.5
5th quintile	3.3	3.3	3.3	3.1	3.1	3

Source: GAO analysis of DOT data.

Table 7. Market Concentration by Airport-Pair Market Size, as Measured by the Herfindahl-Hirschman Index

	2007	2008	2009	2010	2011	2012
1st quintile	4,910	4,783	4,547	4,549	4,295	4,202
2nd quintile	5,311	5,334	5,408	5,411	5,237	5,372
3rd quintile	5,831	5,825	5,816	5,654	5,722	5,693
4th quintile	5,389	5,306	5,343	5,450	5,419	5,490
5th quintile	5,049	5,082	5,023	5,173	5,259	5,375

Source: GAO analysis of DOT data.

Table 8. Market Concentration by City-Pair Market Size, as Measured by the Herfindahl-Hirschman Index

	2007	2008	2009	2010	2011	2012
1st quintile	3,352	3,362	3,240	3,288	3,093	3,196
2nd quintile	3,611	3,636	3,618	3,599	3,551	3,451
3rd quintile	3,981	4,021	3,956	3,957	3,952	4,022
4th quintile	4,377	4,351	4,341	4,432	4,469	4,476
5th quintile	4,944	4,876	4,845	4,985	5,064	5,152

Source: GAO analysis of DOT data.

End Notes

[1] Network (or the Airline Deregulation Act of 1978 (Pub. L. No. 95-504, 92 Stat. 1705) and provide service through hubs from "anywhere to everywhere." For purposes of this report we have defined Alaska Airlines, American Airlines, Continental Airlines, Delta Air Lines, Hawaiian Airlines, Northwest Airlines, United Airlines and US Airways as network airlines.

[2] Low-cost airlines generally entered the market after deregulation and tend to operate point-to-point service. We have defined AirTran Airways, Allegiant Air, America West Airlines, Frontier Airlines, JetBlue, Southwest Airlines, Spirit Airlines, and Virgin America as low-cost airlines.

[3] We used Department of Transportation (DOT) T-100 data for domestic marketing airlines in 2013 to determine industry market share. According to DOT, the marketing airline issues a flight reservation or ticket either on their aircraft or under a code-share agreement with another airline that may provide the actual transportation.

[4] In general, federal statute defines large-hub airports as those commercial service airports that have at least 1 percent of the passenger boardings. Medium- and small-hub airports are defined as having between .25 and 1 percent, and .05 and .25 percent, respectively. Nonhub airports enplaned at least 10,000 passengers, but no more than .05 percent of all passenger boardings. 49 U.S.C. § 40102(29),(31),(42).

[5] Under a capacity purchase agreement, network airlines contract with regional airlines to provide air service beyond the network airline's route network to increase their capacity and revenue. Agreement terms vary, but network airlines generally take on all commercial functions, such as brand marketing, flight scheduling, and ticket pricing, while the regional airlines are responsible for the aircraft and crews to operate the flights and provide ground and flight operations.

[6] GAO, *Commercial Aviation: Airline Industry Contraction Due to Volatile Fuel Prices and Falling Demand Affects Airports, Passengers, and Federal Government Revenues*, GAO-09-393 (Washington, D.C.: Apr. 21, 2009).

[7] A Chapter 7 proceeding is a court-supervised procedure by which a trustee takes over the debtor's assets, reduces them to cash, and makes distributions to creditors. Debtors that are commercial enterprises desiring continuation of some or all of the debtor's operations ordinarily seek to reorganize under Chapter 11 as a way to satisfy creditor claims. Under Chapter 11, typically the debtor remains in control of the assets. If, however, the bankruptcy court determines that this is not in the best interest of creditors, the court can appoint a trustee to oversee the debtor.

[8] Mergers generally refer to the combination of two companies into one company by mutual consent, while acquisitions (also called takeovers) refer to one company's purchase of assets or equity in another company on friendly or hostile terms.

[9] GAO, *Airline Mergers: Issues Raised by the Proposed Merger of American Airlines and US Airways*, GAO-13-403T (Washington, D.C.: June 19, 2013).

[10] GAO, *Airline Mergers: Issues Raised by the Proposed Merger of United and Continental Airlines*, GAO-10-778T (Washington, D.C.: May 27, 2010).

[11] For the purpose of this analysis, an effective competitor is any airline that carries at least 5 percent of the traffic in a given market.

[12] Some studies have found that greater market concentration is associated with higher prices and, in the context of federal antitrust enforcement, market concentration remains an important predictor of federal agency action. See Jonathan S. Baker and Carl Shapiro, "Reinvigorating Horizontal Merger Enforcement," in *How the Chicago School Overshot the Mark: The Effect of Conservative Economic Analysis on U.S. Antitrust*, ed. by Robert Pitofsky (Oxford University Press: 2008) and Carl Shapiro, "The Horizontal Merger Guidelines: From Hedgehog to Fox in Forty Years," 77 *Antitrust L. J.* 701 (2010). For additional discussion, see William E. Kovacic and Carl Shapiro, "Antitrust Policy: A Century of Economic and Legal Thinking," *Journal of Economic Perspectives*, vol. 14, no. 1 (Winter 2000).

[13] GAO, *Airline Competition: Effects of Airline Market Concentration and Barriers to Entry on Airfares*, GAO/RCED-91-101 (Washington, D.C.: Apr. 26, 1991).

[14] The Guidelines were jointly developed by DOJ's Antitrust Division and the Federal Trade Commission and describe the inquiry process the two agencies follow in analyzing proposed mergers. The current version of the Guidelines was revised in August 2010.

[15] Most proposed airline mergers or acquisitions must be reviewed by DOJ. In particular, under the Hart-Scott-Rodino Antitrust Improvements Act of 1976 (Pub. L. No. 94-435, 90 Stat. 1383), any acquisition of voting securities or assets above a set monetary amount must be reported to DOJ (or the Federal Trade Commission for certain industries) so the Department can determine whether the merger or acquisition raises antitrust concerns. See 15 U.S.C. § 18a(d)(1). DOJ has the lead role in reviewing proposed mergers and acquisitions in the airline industry, given its statutory authority to enforce antitrust laws. DOT also has authority under 15 U.S.C. § 21 to bring administrative proceedings against airline mergers that violate the antitrust laws; however, according to DOT it has not exercised this authority.

[16] HHI is calculated by summing the squares of the individual firms' market shares. In addition to market concentration, DOJ's review of proposed mergers considers (1) the extent of potential adverse competitive effects of the merger, such as whether the merged entity will be able to charge higher prices or restrict output for the product or service it sells; (2) whether other competitors are likely to enter the affected markets and whether they would counteract any potential anticompetitive effects that the merger might have posed; (3) the verified "merger specific" efficiencies or other competitive benefits that may be generated by the merger and that cannot be obtained through any other means; and (4) whether, absent the merger or acquisition, one of the firms is likely to fail, causing its assets to exit the market.

[17] 49 U.S.C. § 41110.

[18] The universe of passenger airlines considered for our analysis accounts for almost all U.S. passengers. For example, it accounts for 99 percent of all passengers flying in the U.S. in the fourth quarter of 2012. It excludes charter and cargo airlines.

[19] A repurchase of stock is a distribution in the form of a company buying back its stock from shareholders.

[20] According to Fitch, the issuer default rating addresses an entity's relative vulnerability to default on financial obligations. "B" ratings indicate that material default risk is present, but a limited margin of safety remains. Firms with "BB" ratings remain vulnerable to default risk, particularly in the event of adverse changes in business or economic conditions over

time; however, business or financial flexibility exists, which supports the servicing of financial commitments. "BBB" ratings represent good credit quality and indicate that expectations of current default risk are low.

[21] GAO-13-403T.

[22] GAO-08-845.

[23] Available seat miles are the number of seats offered by an airplane multiplied by the number of scheduled miles flown. This is a typical measure of capacity in the airline industry.

[24] Unit revenues are the operating revenues airlines earn per available seat mile.

[25] We did not adjust unit revenue and unit cost figures for stage length, which is the average distance flown per aircraft departure. Adjusting for stage length standardizes the inherent differences in route structures among airlines and allows for more even comparisons of unit revenue and cost differences. Although, in general, network airlines have had longer stage lengths than low-cost airlines, average stage length for low-cost airlines, especially Southwest Airlines, has been increasing since 2007 and therefore stage length adjustments have less of an effect.

[26] GAO-08-845.

[27] Charging fees for services is also known as unbundling charges, offering a la carte pricing, or charging ancillary fees. See GAO, *Commercial Aviation: Consumers Could Benefit from Better Information about Airline-Imposed Fees and Refundability of Government-Imposed Taxes and Fees*, GAO-10-785 (Washington, D.C.: July 14, 2010).

[28] Specifically, DOT only requires airlines to report excess baggage and reservation change fees in separate accounts; other ancillary fees are commingled with other revenue accounts.

[29] GAO-08-845.

[30] The Pension Benefit Guarantee Corporation was established under the Employee Retirement Income Security Act of 1974 (ERISA) (Pub. L. No. 93-406, 88 Stat. 829, 1003) and set forth standards and requirements that apply to defined benefit plans. It was established to encourage the continuation and maintenance of voluntary private pension plans and to insure the benefits of workers and retirees in defined benefit plans should plan sponsors fail to pay benefits. The corporation's operations are financed, for example, by insurance premiums paid by sponsors of defined benefit plans, investment income, and assets from pension plans trusted by the corporation, and recoveries from the companies formerly responsible for the plans. See GAO, *Airline Mergers: Issues Raised by the Proposed Merger of American Airlines and US Airways,* GAO-13-403T (Washington, D.C.: June 19, 2013). During bankruptcy, United and US Airways terminated their pension plans and shifted $9.7 billion in claims to the corporation. As a result, plan participants lost $5.3 billion in benefits (in constant 2005 dollars). See GAO, *Commercial Aviation: Bankruptcy and Pension Problems are Symptoms of Underlying Structural Issues,* GAO-05-945 (Washington, D.C.: Sept. 30, 2005).

[31] GAO-08-845.

[32] The cost of fuel for airlines reflects both the price of fuel at any given time and airline fuel hedging strategies. Airlines have used fuel hedges—contracts that are designed to provide more certainty over the future price of fuel—to reduce the effects of fuel price volatility on their earnings. However, airlines incurred substantial losses because of the downside risk to their hedges (i.e., exposure to financial losses) when fuel prices fell in 2008. For example, Southwest's average fuel cost per gallon, including hedging, increased 35.6 percent in 2008 and contributed to a $342 million, or 43.2 percent, decrease in the company's operating income that year.

[33] Bank of America Merrill Lynch, *Airlines Primer: Changing dynamics improve supply discipline*, by Glenn D. Engel and David van der Keyl (New York: 2013).

[34] Gerassimos Tsoukalas, Peter Belobaba, and William Swelbar, "Cost Convergence in the US Airline Industry: An Analysis of Unit Costs 1995-2006," *Journal of Air Transport Management*, vol.14 (2008).

[35] To compare costs across airline segments, we excluded (1) transport-related expenses, as these are primarily payments made by network airlines to regional airlines for service to smaller cities on their behalf, and (2) fuel expenses, as reported fuel costs are not always comparable due to the use of fuel hedging strategies.

[36] Bank of America Merrill Lynch, *Airlines Primer: Changing dynamics improve supply discipline*.

[37] Tsoukalas, Belobaba, and Swelbar, "Cost Convergence in the US Airline Industry."

[38] These are the same minimum passenger counts we have used as a threshold for our analyses in previous reports. We excluded Alaskan and Hawaiian destinations because cost and competitive conditions involving these destinations are likely to be considerably different than routes within the continental U.S.

[39] While this analysis retained 94 percent of all passengers, it only retained 14 percent of the routes as defined by a specific combination of two endpoint airports after applying the passenger-count filter screen. As we noted, data on routes with very few passengers are not robust enough to ensure statistical accuracy. Moreover, such cases may be indicative of errors in the data, or routes that are travelled so rarely that they are not representative of the industry more broadly and are thus not appropriate to include in this analysis.

[40] If there was more than one airport in a metropolitan area, we aggregated traffic from those airports. Thus, for the New York City to Chicago city-pair market, all traffic between the two major commercial airports in Chicago and the three major commercial airports in the New York City area were aggregated to include all city-pair traffic.

[41] As previously noted, we define an effective competitor as any airline that carries at least 5 percent of the traffic in a given market.

[42] To further assess trends in the smallest markets, we also categorized the markets into quintiles based on the total number of markets—rather than by passengers—in our sample. As such, each quintile contained 20 percent of the total *markets*, but the corresponding number of *passengers* in each quintile differed. For instance, each quintile contained about 2,087 markets in 2012, but the first quintile contained about 367 million passengers or about 89 percent of the total, while the fifth quintile contained about 3 million passengers or less than one percent of all passengers. When analyzed this way, we found that the average number of effective competitors in the smallest markets represented in this fifth quintile had fallen only slightly from 2.2 in 2007 to 2.1 in 2012.

[43] When we evaluated the number of monopoly markets using airport-pairs as the relevant market definition, we found similar results. For example, nearly all of the monopoly markets were found in the least-traveled markets and the percentage of monopolies in the most-heavily traveled markets decreased from about .08 percent in 2007 to about .05 percent in 2012.

[44] For example, a market consisting of four firms—two of which have market shares of 30 percent and two of which have market shares of 20 percent—has an HHI of 2,600 ($30 + 30^2 + 20^2 + 20^2 = 2,600$). Although it is desirable to include all firms in the calculation, information about firms with small shares is not critical because such firms do not affect the HHI significantly.

[45] As mentioned previously, we also categorized the markets into quintiles based on the total number of markets—rather than by passengers—in our sample. When analyzed this way, we found that the smallest markets represented in the fifth quintile were much more concentrated than the largest markets in the first quintile and concentration as measured by the HHI increased from 2009 through 2012.

[46] Several competitors on the Salt Lake City-Memphis route had less than 5 percent market share and therefore were not included in our analysis.

[47] GAO-10-778T.

[48] GAO-13-403T.

[49] Similarly, in July 2008, we found that longer-distance markets are more competitive than shorter-distance markets. See GAO-08-845.

[50] The groups of large-, medium-, and small-hub airports in this analysis are based on 2012 data. We used the same group of airports for each year from 2007-2012 in order to compare across years.

[51] Specifically, larger airports with the most passenger traffic experienced about a 14.5 percent reduction in concentration, driven by an increase in the number of competitors in these markets from 2007 to 2012. Most of those increases are due to low-cost airline entry. For smaller airports, concentration levels generally remained flat or increased slightly. For airports in the smallest quintile, for example, the HHI increased about 6 percent from 2007 to 2012.

[52] See Michael D. Wittman and William S. Swelbar, *Evolving Trends of U.S. Domestic Airfares: The Impacts of Competition, Consolidation, and Low-Cost Carriers*, Massachusetts Institute of Technology International Center for Air Transportation (Aug. 2013).

[53] Prior studies have demonstrated the effect of airline competition on airfares and shown that the presence of low-cost airlines in a market is associated with lower fares for all passengers in that market. For a recent comprehensive analysis of airline competition and domestic airfares, see Jan K. Brueckner, Darin Lee, and Ethan S. Singer, "Airline Competition and Domestic U.S. Airfares: A Comprehensive Reappraisal," *Economics of Transportation*, vol. 2 (2013). See also John Kwoka, Kevin Hearle, and Phillippe Alepin, "Segmented Competition in Airlines: The Changing Role of Low-Cost and Legacy Carriers in Fare Determination," *Social Science Research Network* (2013); Mehdi Ben Abda, Peter Belobaba, and William Swelbar, "Impacts of LCC Growth on Domestic Traffic and Fares at Largest U.S. Airports," *Journal of Air Transport Management*, vol. 18 (2012); Steven Morrison, "Actual, Adjacent, and Potential Competition: Estimating the Full Effect of Southwest Airlines," *Journal of Transport Economics and Policy*, vol. 35 (2001); and Martin Dresner, Jiun-Sheng Chris Lin and Robert Windle, "The Impact of Low-Cost Carriers on Airport and Route Competition," *Journal of Transport Economics and Policy*, vol. 30 (1996).

[54] DOJ and DOT's analysis of merger impacts have relied on an expectation that entry by low-cost airlines, especially Southwest Airlines, would check airline fare increases following a merger. We found recently that Southwest expansion has slowed and its acquisition of Air Tran, a low-cost rival, may challenge post-merger fare increases. See GAO-13-403T.

[55] Wittman and Swelbar, *Evolving Trends of U.S. Domestic Airfares*.

[56] Jan K. Brueckner, Darin N. Lee, Pierre M. Picard, and Ethan Singer, "Product Unbundling in the Travel Industry: The Economics of Airline Bag Fees," *Journal of Economics and Management Strategy* (Forthcoming). The study tested the hypothesis that, other things being equal, fares are lower after the adoption of bag fees than before and showed business fares are less affected than leisure fares by the imposition of bag fees.

[57] GAO, *Commercial Aviation: Consumers Could Benefit from Better Information about Airline-Imposed Fees and Refundability of Government-Imposed Taxes and Fees*, GAO-10-785 (Washington, D.C.: July 14, 2010).

[58] GAO, *Commercial Aviation: Status of Air Service to Small Communities and the Federal Programs Involved*, GAO-14-454T (Washington, D.C.: Apr. 30, 2014).

[59] Michael D. Wittman and William S. Swelbar, *Trends and Market Forces Shaping Small Community Air Service in the United States*, Massachusetts Institute of Technology International Center for Air Transportation (May 2013).

[60] See GAO, *Airline Passenger Protections: More Data and Analysis Needed to Understand Effects of Flight Delays*, GAO-11-733 (Washington, D.C.: Sept. 7, 2011).

[61] Lance Sherry, "Passenger Trip Delay Statistics for 2010," *Transportation Research Board*, 2012.

[62] Load factors represent the proportion of airline output that is actually consumed and are calculated by dividing revenue passenger miles by available seat miles.

[63] The DOT Inspector General (IG) has recently found that when airline markets became less competitive both the average length of flight delays and percentage of late flights increased.

See DOT IG *Reductions in Competition Increase Airline Flight Delays and Cancellations*, CR-2014-040 (Washington, D.C.: Apr. 23, 2014).

[64] GAO-10-778T.

[65] Funding for airport capital development comes from four primary sources: federal Airport Improvement Program (AIP) grants, passenger facility charges (PFCs), municipal bonds, and state and local grants. Airports vary in their reliance on these sources of funds. The Federal Aviation Administration allocates most AIP grants on the basis of (1) a legislated apportionment formula tied to the number of passengers an airport enplanes in the case of primary airports, and (2) set-aside categories earmarked for specific types of airports and projects. PFCs, which are collected from passengers, were introduced in 1990 to finance local airport infrastructure projects at commercial airports. In 2000, the Wendell H. Ford Aviation Investment and Reform Act for the 21 Century (AIR-21) raised the cap on PFCs from $3.00 to $4.50 per boarding passenger. Pub. L. No. 106-181, § 105, 114 Stat.61, 71 (2000). Airports have long sought to increase the PFC cap, arguing that it has not been adjusted for inflation, but airlines oppose any PFC rate increase that inhibits the demand for air travel.

[66] Wittman and Swelbar, *Trends and Market Forces Shaping Small Community Air Service in the United States*.

[67] Slot controls are limits imposed by FAA through regulations or orders on the number of takeoffs and landings airlines may make per hour at Ronald Reagan Washington National Airport in Washington, D.C., and the three major airports in the New York metropolitan area: John F. Kennedy International, LaGuardia, and Newark Liberty International Airports.

[68] GAO, *Slot-Controlled Airports: FAA's Rules Could be Improved to Enhance Competition and Use of Available Capacity*, GAO-12-902 (Washington, D.C.: Sept. 13, 2012).

[69] Existing slot control rules require airlines to operate their slots at least 80 percent of the time, which allows airlines not to schedule some of their allocated slots. 14 C.F.R. Part 93, subparts K and S; 76 Fed. Reg. 18618 (Apr. 4, 2011); 76 Fed. Reg. 18616 (Apr. 4, 2011); 76 Fed. Reg. 18620 (Apr. 4, 2011).

[70] Majority-in-interest clauses are provisions in an airport's general use agreement with an airline that typically give those airlines performing a majority of the operations at the airport veto power over airport expansion when those airlines would be responsible for paying the cost of that expansion.

[71] Airports affected by the settlement include Washington Reagan National Airport, LaGuardia Airport, Boston Logan International Airport, Chicago O'Hare International Airport, Dallas Love Field, Los Angeles International Airport, and Miami International Airport. See "*United States of America, et al. v. US Airways Group, Inc. and AMR Corporation*," No. 1:13-cv-01236 (D.D.C., Apr. 25, 2014).

[72] DOT Report on Significant Rulemakings, available at http://www.dot.gov/regulations/report-on-significant-rulemakings, April 2014.

[73] 49 U.S.C. §§ 40117(k), 47106(f); FAA Program Guidance Letter 04-08 (Sept. 30, 2004).

[74] Mara Lederman, "Are Frequent Flyer Programs a Cause of the 'Hub Premium?'" *Journal of Economics & Management Strategy*, vol.17 (2008).

[75] Department of Transportation Office of the Secretary, Final Rule, "Enhancing Airline Passenger Protections," 76 Fed. Reg. 23110 (Apr. 25, 2011). Legislation introduced recently in Congress would require DOT to issue a final regulation to allow airlines to disclose federal taxes and fees separately from the base airfare. Transparent Airfares Act of 2014, H.R. 4156, 113th Cong. (2014).

[76] GAO-10-785.

[77] GAO-10-785.

[78] DOT issued the Notice of Proposed Rulemaking for the third Enhancing Airline Passenger Protections rule in May 2014. Among other requirements, DOT proposes to require airlines and ticket agents to disclose at all points of sale the fees for certain basic ancillary services

associated with the air transportation consumers are buying or considering buying, including first and second checked bags, one carry-on item, and advanced seat selection. Department of Transportation Office of the Secretary, Notice of Proposed Rulemaking, "Transparency of Airline Ancillary Fees and Other Consumer Protection Issues," 79 Fed. Reg. 29970 (May 23, 2014).

[79] Department of Transportation Office of the Secretary, Notice of Proposed Rulemaking, "Reporting Ancillary Airline Passenger Revenues," 76 Fed. Reg. 41726 (July 15, 2011).

[80] The International Air Transport Association (IATA) represents the global airline industry and is responsible for establishing standards in many areas of the airline business, including airline ticketing and baggage, that make it possible for passengers to travel from one place to another using two or more airlines. IATA also leads a number of industry initiatives involving safety, security, environment, and passenger rights.

[81] Order to Show Cause (Order 2014-5-7). Agreement among Member Carriers of the International Air Transport Association concerning an agreement (Resolution 787) of the Passenger Services Conference, Docket OST-2013-0048 (Department of Transportation, May 21, 2014).

[82] Pursuant to the Antitrust Procedures and Penalties Act (Pub. L. No. 93-528, 88 Stat. 1706 (1974) (codified at 15 U.S.C. § 16), also known as the Tunney Act, the American Antitrust Institute, AirlinePassengers.org, Association for Airline Passenger Rights, Business Travel Coalition, Consumer Travel Alliance, and FlyersRights.org filed comments to object to the settlement of the case of *United States v. US Airways Group Inc. and AMR Corp.*, No. 1:13-cv-01236 (CKK), claiming that it was not in the public interest (Washington, D.C.: Feb. 7, 2014).

[83] Major airlines worldwide have joined one of three major international alliances— SkyTeam, Star Alliance, and oneworld—to extend their network to foreign countries.

[84] DOT considers a wide range of factors in evaluating whether a transaction is in the public interest, including the availability of a variety of air service, maximum reliance on market forces, the avoidance of unreasonable industry concentration, and opportunities for the expansion of international services. Because each alliance case presents a unique set of circumstances and because the industry environment changes rapidly, the public interest standard is applied on a case-by-case basis. 49 U.S.C. §§§ 41309(b), 41308(b) and 40101(a).

[85] Transportation Research Board National Research Council, *Entry and Competition in the U.S. Airline Industry: Issues and Opportunities*, Special Report 255 (Washington, D.C.: 1999).

[86] The U.S. also has ownership restrictions relating to the navigation of aircraft in the United States. 49 U.S.C. §§ 41102 and 40102(a)(15); In the Matter of the Acquisition of Northwest Airlines, Inc. by Wings, DOT Order 91-1-41, Docket No. 46371 (Jan. 1991).

[87] U.S. Department of Transportation, *The Future of Aviation Advisory Committee Final Report* (Washington, D.C.: Apr. 11, 2011).

[88] GAO-12-902.

[89] IRS Announcement 2002-18, "Frequent Flyer Miles Attributable to Business or Official Travel" (2002). The 2002 Announcement provides, in part, that "IRS will not assert that any taxpayer has understated his federal tax liability by reason of the receipt or personal use of frequent flyer miles or other in-kind promotional benefits attributable to the taxpayer's business or official travel."

[90] See 49 U.S.C. § 41713.

[91] See e.g., *Morales v. Trans World Airlines, Inc.*, 504 U.S. 374 (1992). The *Morales* Court noted, however, that "some state actions may affect [airline rates or services] in too tenuous, remote, or peripheral a manner" to be preempted. *Id.* at 388, 112 S. Ct. at 2040 (quoting *Shaw v. Delta Airlines, Inc.*, 463 U.S. 85, 100 n. 21, 103 S. Ct. 2890, 2901, n. 21, 77 L. Ed. 2d 490 (1983)).

[92] Although America West merged with US Airways in 2005, it still reported as a separate entity in 2007.

[93] While this analysis retained 94 percent of all passengers, it only retained 14 percent of the routes as defined by a specific combination of two endpoint airports after applying the passenger count filter screen. As we noted, data on routes with very few passengers are not robust enough to ensure statistical accuracy. Moreover, such cases may be indicative of errors in the data, or routes that are travelled so rarely that they are not representative of the industry more broadly and are thus not appropriate to include in this analysis.

[94] See GAO-13-403T, GAO-08-845, and GAO-10-778T.

[95] For comparison purposes we also created a separate market-level data-set based on city-pairs as defined in Jan Brueckner, Darin Lee, and Ethan Singer, "City-Pair Versus Airport-Pairs: A Market Definition Methodology for the Airline Industry," *Review of Industrial Organization*, vol. 44 (2014). The results were generally consistent with what we found using DOT's methodology for grouping city-pair markets.

In: Airline Competition and Consolidation
Editor: Caroline Reid
ISBN: 978-1-63463-119-8

Chapter 2

AIRLINE MERGERS: ISSUES RAISED BY THE PROPOSED MERGER OF AMERICAN AIRLINES AND US AIRWAYS. STATEMENT OF GERALD L. DILLINGHAM, DIRECTOR, PHYSICAL INFRASTRUCTURE ISSUES, GOVERNMENT ACCOUNTABILITY OFFICE. HEARING ON "AIRLINE INDUSTRY CONSOLIDATION"*

WHY GAO DID THIS STUDY

In February 2013, American and US Airways announced plans to merge the two airlines and entered into a merger agreement. Valued at $11 billion, the merged airline would retain the American name and be headquartered in Dallas-Fort Worth. This follows the mergers of United Airlines and Continental Airlines in 2010 and the acquisition of Northwest Airlines by Delta Air Lines (Delta) in 2008. This latest merger, if not challenged by DOJ, would surpass these prior mergers in scope to create the largest passenger airline in the United States. The passenger airline industry has struggled financially over the last decade and these two airlines believe a merger will

* This is an edited, reformatted and augmented version of testimony presented June 19, 2013 before the Senate Committee on Commerce, Science and Transportation, Subcommittee on Aviation Operations, Safety, and Security.

strengthen them. However, as with any merger of this magnitude, this proposal will be examined by DOJ to determine if its potential benefits for consumers outweigh the potential negative effects.

This testimony focuses on (1) the role of federal authorities in reviewing merger proposals, (2) key factors motivating airline mergers in recent years, and (3) the implications of merging American and US Airways. To address these objectives, GAO drew from its previous reports on the potential effects of prior airline mergers and the financial condition of the airline industry issued from July 2008 through May 2010. GAO also analyzed DOT's airline operating and financial data, airline financial documents, and airline schedule information since 2002.

What GAO Found

The Department of Justice's (DOJ) antitrust review will be a critical step in the proposed merger between American Airlines (American) and US Airways. DOJ uses an integrated analytical framework set forth in the *Horizontal Merger Guidelines* to determine whether the merger poses any antitrust concerns. Under that process, DOJ assesses, among other things, the extent of likely anticompetitive effects of the proposed merger in the relevant markets, in this case, airline city-pair markets, and the likelihood that other airlines may enter these markets and counteract any anticompetitive effects, such as higher fares. DOJ also considers efficiencies that a merger or acquisition could bring—for example, consumer benefits from an expanded route network. The Department of Transportation (DOT) aids DOJ's analysis.

Airlines seek mergers to reduce costs and improve revenues. GAO has previously reported that mergers can result in increased revenues by offering improved network connections and schedules, but also through higher fares on some routes. Cost savings can be generated by eliminating redundancies and operational efficiencies, including reducing service, but can be muted by problems in combining different aircraft, technologies, and labor forces. In the case of US Airways and American, they estimate that a merger would yield $1.4 billion in annual benefits from increased revenues and reduced costs.

If not challenged by DOJ, the merged American would surpass United to become the largest U.S. passenger airline by several measures. While US Airways and American overlap on only 12 nonstop routes, no other nonstop competitors exist on 7 of those 12. Our analysis of 2011 and 2012 ticket data also showed that combining these airlines would result in a loss of one effective competitor (defined as having at least 5 percent of total airport-pair traffic) in 1,665 airport-pair markets affecting more than 53 million passengers while creating a new effective competitor in 210 airport-pairs affecting 17.5 million passengers. However, the great majority of these markets also have other effective competitors.

Chairman Cantwell, Ranking Member Ayotte, and Members of the Subcommittee:

I am pleased to be here today to discuss the potential implications of the merger proposal recently announced by American Airlines (American) and US Airways. In February 2013, these two airlines announced plans for American to merge with US Airways through a stock swap the airlines valued at $11 billion. This follows the acquisition of Northwest Airlines (Northwest) by Delta Air Lines (Delta) in 2008, the merger of United Airlines (United) and Continental Airlines (Continental) in 2010, and Southwest Airlines' (Southwest) acquisition of Air Tran Airways (AirTran), in 2011. If approved by the Department of Justice (DOJ), the American-US Airways merger would surpass United's in terms of number of employees, seat capacity, and operating revenues to create the largest passenger airline in the United States. However, as with any merger of this magnitude, this proposal is being examined by DOJ with assistance from the Department of Transportation (DOT) to determine if the potential benefits for consumers outweigh the potential negative effects.

Extensive research and the experience of millions of Americans underscore the benefits that have flowed to most consumers from the 1978 deregulation of the airline industry, including dramatic reductions in fares and expansion of service. These benefits are largely attributable to increased competition from the entry of new airlines into the industry and established airlines into new markets. At the same time, however, airline deregulation has not benefited everyone; some communities—especially smaller communities—have suffered from relatively high airfares and a loss of service. We have been analyzing aviation competition issues since enactment of the Airline Deregulation Act of 1978.[1] Our work since 2000 has focused on airline competition and industry performance, including the financial health of the passenger airline industry, the growth of low cost airlines, changing business models of airlines, and prior mergers.[2] In the airline context, DOJ has the primary responsibility to evaluate most mergers in order to carry out its antitrust responsibilities.[3] In addition, American remains under Chapter 11 bankruptcy protection, however the bankruptcy court approved the merger with US Airways in May 2013.

My statement today presents the (1) role of federal authorities in reviewing merger proposals, (2) key factors motivating airline mergers in recent years, and (3) implications of merging American and US Airways. My testimony is based on several reports we previously prepared for this Committee—our 2008 report on the potential effects of the proposed merger between Delta and Northwest and our 2009 report on the financial condition of the airline industry and the various effects of the industry's contraction on passengers and communities—as well as our 2010 Statement for this Committee on the United-Continental merger[4] and other past work on aviation issues since 2000. In addition, we conducted analysis of the proposed American and US Airways merger, including some analysis of the airlines' financial, labor, fleet, and market conditions. To describe the role of federal authorities, in particular DOJ and DOT, in reviewing airline merger proposals we relied on information developed for our 2008 report and updated it as necessary.[5] For example, we reviewed new merger guidelines issued in 2010 and recent merger decisions. To provide an overview of the factors motivating airline mergers in recent years, we relied on information developed from past reports on the airline industry and updated it as necessary.[6] For example, we reviewed American Airlines bankruptcy and merger documents. To identify the implications of the proposed merger of American and US Airways, we reviewed airline documents about the merger, financial analyst reports, and analyzed data submitted by the airlines to DOT since 2002 (BTS Form 41 financial data, origin and destination ticket sample, and operations). We also analyzed airline schedule data. We assessed the reliability of these data by (1) performing electronic testing of required data elements, (2) reviewing existing information about the data and the system that produced them, and (3) interviewing agency officials knowledgeable about the data. We determined that the data were sufficiently reliable for the purposes of this testimony.

We conducted this work in accordance with generally accepted government auditing standards. Those standards require that we plan and perform the audit to obtain sufficient, appropriate evidence to provide a reasonable basis for our findings and conclusions based on our audit objectives. We believe that the evidence obtained provides a reasonable basis for our findings and conclusions based on our audit objectives.

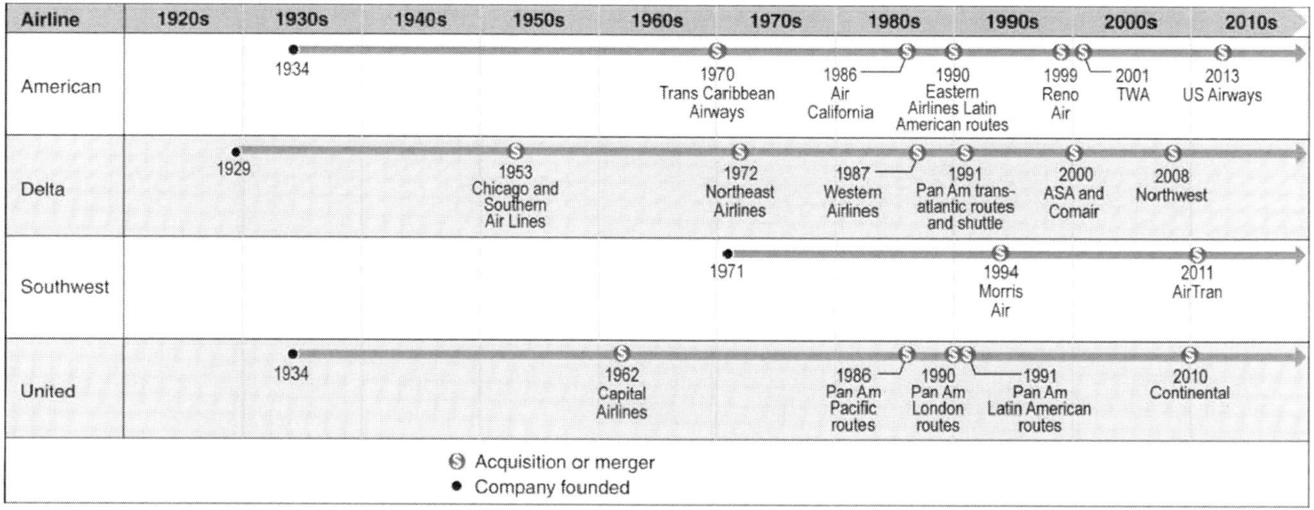

Sources: Cathay Financial and airline company documents.

Figure 1. Highlights of Domestic Airline Mergers and Acquisitions, 1920s – 2010s.

BACKGROUND

The airline industry has experienced considerable merger and acquisition activity since its early years; especially immediately following deregulation in 1978. Figure 1 provides a timeline of mergers and acquisitions for the four largest surviving airlines, assuming an American–US Airways merger, based on passengers served. A flurry of mergers and acquisitions occurred during the 1980s, when Delta and Western Airlines merged, United acquired Pan Am's Pacific routes, Northwest acquired Republic Airlines, and American and Air California merged. In 1988, merger and acquisition review authority was transferred from DOT to DOJ.[7] Since 2000, American acquired the bankrupt airline TWA in 2001, America West acquired US Airways in 2005, while the latter was in bankruptcy; Delta acquired Northwest in 2008; United acquired Continental in 2010; and Southwest acquired AirTran in 2011. Certain other attempts at merging since 2000 failed because of opposition from DOJ or employees and creditors. For example, in 2000, an agreement was reached that allowed Northwest to acquire a 50 percent stake in Continental (with limited voting power) to resolve the antitrust suit brought by DOJ against Northwest's proposed acquisition of a controlling interest in Continental.[8] A proposed merger of United and US Airways in 2000 also resulted in opposition from DOJ, which found that in its view, the merger would violate antitrust laws by reducing competition, increasing air fares, and harming consumers on airline routes throughout the United States. Although DOJ expressed its intent to sue to block the transaction, the parties abandoned the transaction before a suit was filed. In 2006, the proposed merger of US Airways and Delta fell apart because of opposition from Delta's pilots and some of its creditors, as well as its senior management.

Since deregulation in 1978, the financial stability of the airline industry has become a considerable concern for the federal government due, in part, to the level of financial assistance it has provided to the industry through assuming terminated pension plans and other forms of assistance. From 1979 through 2012, there have been at least 194 airline bankruptcies, according to Airlines for America (A4A), an airline trade group. While most of these bankruptcies affected small airlines that were eventually liquidated, 4 of the more recent bankruptcies prior to American's (Delta, Northwest, United, and US Airways) are among the largest corporate bankruptcies ever, excluding financial services firms. During these bankruptcies, United and US Airways terminated the defined benefit pension plans for their labor groups and $9.7 billion in claims were shifted to the Pension Benefit Guarantee Corporation

(PGBC).[9] Further, to respond to the financial shock to the industry from the September 11, 2001, terrorist attacks, the federal government provided airlines with $7.4 billion in direct assistance and authorized $1.6 billion (of $10 billion available) in loan guarantees to six airlines.[10]

Although the airline industry has experienced numerous mergers and bankruptcies since deregulation, growth of existing airlines and the entry of new airlines have contributed to a steady increase in capacity, as measured by available seat miles. Previously, we reported that although one airline may reduce capacity or leave the market, capacity returns relatively quickly through new airline entry and expansion of the remaining airlines.[11] However, in recent years this dynamic may be changing. Domestic capacity growth stalled in 2008 owing to the recession and high fuel prices and has not rebounded despite a strengthening economy and demand for air travel (see figure 2).

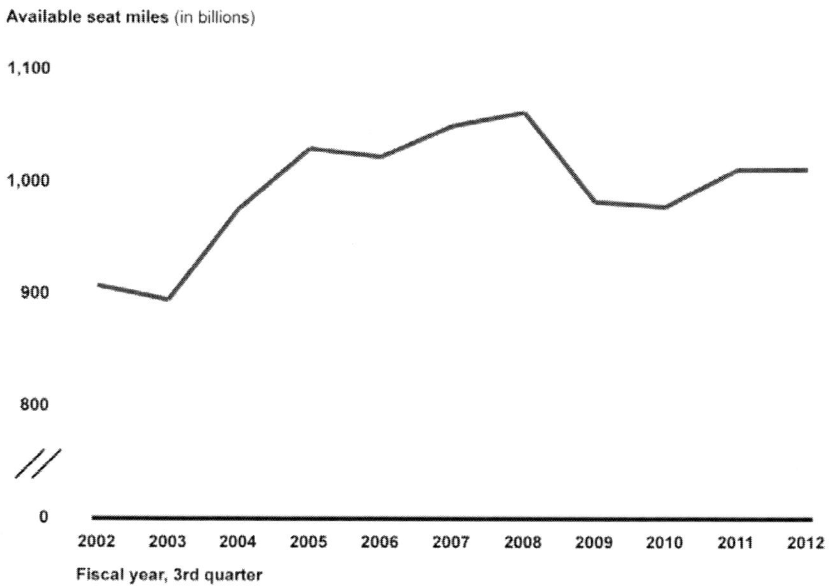

Source: GAO analysis of DOT data.

Figure 2. Domestic Passenger Airline Capacity (Fiscal Years 2002 to 2012, Third Quarter).

In recent years, a key factor limiting capacity growth has been high fuel prices, according to industry analysts. In the early part of the last decade while network airlines[12] were restructuring their costs through bankruptcy, low cost airlines like Southwest and JetBlue expanded owing to lower costs, especially for labor (see figure 3). As a result, while in 2002, network airlines offered 67 percent of domestic seat capacity versus 23 percent for low cost airlines, by October 2012, network airlines share of domestic seats had fallen to 52 percent and low cost airline's share had risen to 33 percent. However, the expansion of low cost airlines in recent years may have slowed owing to higher fuel costs that diminished their relative cost advantage over network airlines. With fuel costs consuming a greater proportion of airline operating costs for all airlines, any cost advantage that low cost airlines had with respect to labor costs over network airlines is diluted.

Finally, DOJ and DOT's analysis of merger impacts have relied on an expectation that entry by low cost airlines, especially Southwest, would check airline fare increases following a merger. However, that practice might erode as Southwest expansion has slowed and it recently merged with a key low cost rival, reducing the number of low cost airlines that might challenge post merger fare increases. In 1993, DOT published a report entitled the The Southwest Effect that concluded that low cost airlines like Southwest lowered fares in markets they entered and that DOT policy should be to encourage the growth of Southwest and airlines like it.[13] Congressional action and DOT policy in subsequent years, especially in the award of operating rights called "slots" at congested airports like Washington Reagan and New York LaGuardia, favored new entrant airlines like Southwest. Similarly, DOJ cited the relinquishment of 36 slots by Continental to Southwest at Newark Liberty International Airport as alleviating its principle concerns in determining not to object to the United–Continental merger in 2010. A November 2008 paper by Goolsbee and Syverson, found that even the threat of entry by Southwest in a market helped to lower fares in that market, but only if Southwest already operated at one of the market endpoints.[14] More recently though, a 2013 study suggests that the Southwest Effect may not be as prominent following a merger. This study found that Southwest raised fares in markets following the mergers of Delta–Northwest and US Airways– America West more than average fare increases overall, unless another low cost airline was already in that market.[15] The merger of Southwest with a key rival in 2011 could further lessen the potential that Southwest would deter or counteract higher fares in markets following a merger.

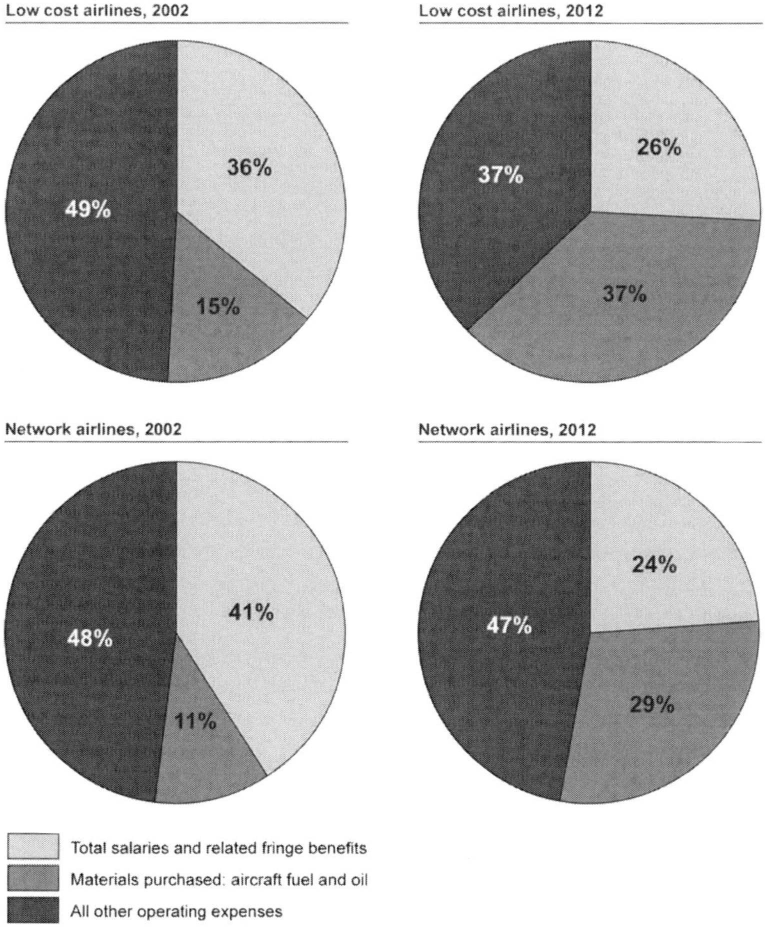

Source: GAO analysis of DOT Form 41 data.

Figure 3. Total Operating Costs (Fiscal Years 2002 and 2012, Third Quarter).

The Department of Justice's Antitrust Review Is a Critical Step in the Airline Merger and Acquisition Process

The DOJ's review of airline mergers and acquisitions is a key step for airlines hoping to consummate a merger. For airlines, as with other industries,

DOJ uses an analytical framework set forth in the Horizontal Merger Guidelines (the Guidelines) to evaluate merger proposals.[16] In addition, DOT plays an advisory role for DOJ and, if the combination is consummated, may conduct financial and safety reviews of the combined entity under its regulatory authority.[17] Finally, because American has been under Chapter 11 bankruptcy protection since 2011, the merger also required federal bankruptcy court approval.

Most proposed airline mergers or acquisitions must be reviewed by DOJ as required by the Hart-Scott-Rodino Antitrust Improvements Act (Act).[18] In particular, under the Act, an acquisition of voting securities or assets above a set monetary amount must be reported to DOJ (or the FTC for certain industries) so the department can determine whether the merger or acquisition poses any antitrust concerns.[19] To analyze whether a proposed merger or acquisition raises antitrust concerns—whether the proposal will likely create, enhance, or entrench "market power" or facilitate its exercise[20]—DOJ follows an analytical process set forth in the Guidelines.[21] The commentary to the Guidelines identifies five factors that the department considers in reviewing a merger but notes that their importance varies according to the nature of the industry and the scope of the merger. The five factors considered by DOJ are:

- the relevant product and geographic markets in which the companies operate and whether the merger is likely to significantly increase concentration in those markets, which in the case of airlines principally applies to city-pair markets;
- the extent of potential adverse competitive effects of the merger, such as whether the merged entity will be able to charge higher prices or restrict output for the product or service it sells;
- whether other competitors are likely to enter the affected markets and whether they would counteract any potential anticompetitive effects that the merger might have posed;
- the verified "merger specific" efficiencies or other competitive benefits that may be generated by the merger and that cannot be obtained through any other means; and
- whether, absent the merger or acquisition, one of the firms is likely to fail, causing its assets to exit the market.

In making the decision whether the proposed merger is likely anticompetitive, DOJ considers the particular circumstances of the merger as it relates to the Guidelines' five-part analysis. The greater the potential anticompetitive effects, the greater the offsetting verifiable efficiencies for DOJ to clear a merger must be. However, according to the Guidelines, efficiencies almost never justify a merger if it would create a monopoly or near monopoly. If DOJ concludes that a merged airline threatens to deprive consumers of the benefits of competitive air service, then it will seek injunctive relief in a court proceeding to block the merger from being consummated. For example, a proposed merger of United Airlines and US Airways was opposed by DOJ, which found that, in its view, the merger would violate antitrust laws by reducing competition, increasing air fares, and harming consumers on airline routes throughout the United States. In some cases, the parties may agree to modify the proposal to address anticompetitive concerns identified by DOJ—for example, selling airport assets or giving up slots at congested airports—in which case DOJ ordinarily files a complaint with the court along with a consent decree that embodies the agreed-upon changes.

DOT conducts its own analyses of airline mergers and acquisitions. While DOJ is responsible for upholding antitrust laws, DOT reviews the merits of any airline merger or acquisition and submits its views and relevant information in its possession to DOJ. DOT also provides some essential data—for example, the airlines' routes and passenger traffic—that DOJ uses in its review. In addition, presuming the merger moves forward after DOJ's review, DOT can undertake several other reviews if the situation warrants. Before commencing operations, any new, acquired, or merged airlines must obtain separate authorizations from DOT—"economic" authority from the Office of the Secretary[22] and "safety" authority from the Federal Aviation Administration (FAA).[23] The Office of the Secretary is responsible for deciding whether applicants are fit, willing, and able to perform the service or provide transportation. To make this decision, the Secretary assesses whether the applicants have the managerial competence, disposition to comply with regulations, and financial resources necessary to operate a new airline. FAA is responsible for certifying that the aircraft and operations conform to the safety standards prescribed by the Administrator, for instance, that the applicants' manuals, aircraft, facilities, and personnel meet federal safety standards. Also, if a merger or other corporate transaction involves the transfer of international route authority, DOT is responsible for assessing and approving all transfers to ensure that they are consistent with the public interest.[24]

In addition, American has been under federal bankruptcy protection since November 2011.[25] In May 2013, the federal judge overseeing the bankruptcy approved American's merger with US Airways as part of the reorganization.[26]

Shareholders of US Airways must also approve the merger for it to be consummated.

FINANCIAL BENEFITS TO SHAREHOLDERS DRIVE AIRLINE MERGERS

On February 13, 2013, American and US Airways announced an agreement to merge the two airlines. The airlines have also notified DOJ of their intent to merge. The new airline would retain the American name and headquarters in Dallas-Fort Worth while the current US Airways Chief Executive Officer would keep that title with the new airline, and the current American CEO would become Chairman of the new American. The proposed merger will be financed exclusively through an all stock transaction with a combined equity value of $11 billion split roughly with 72 percent ownership to American shareholders and 28 percent to US Airways shareholders. The airlines have not announced specific plans for changes in their networks or operations that would occur if the combination is consummated, but the airlines' conservatively estimate that the merger will result in $1.4 billion in annual benefits to shareholders of the new airline as outlined in table 1.

A key financial benefit that airlines consider in a merger is the potential for increased revenues through additional demand (generated by more seamless travel to more destinations), increased market share, and higher fares on some routes. As we reported in May 2010, mergers may generate additional demand by providing consumers more domestic and international city-pair destinations.[27] Airlines with expansive domestic and international networks and frequent flier benefits particularly appeal to business traffic, especially corporate accounts. The American–US Airways merger is estimated by airline executives to generate $1.12 billion in revenue synergies from improved network connectivity, increased corporate and frequent flier loyalty, and optimization in the use of their aircraft.

At the same time, capacity reductions in certain markets from a merger or acquisition could also serve to generate additional revenue through increased fares on some routes. Some studies of airline mergers and acquisitions during the 1980s showed that prices were higher on some routes from the airline's hubs soon after the combination was completed.[28] Several studies have also shown that increased airline dominance at an airport results in increased fare premiums, in part, because that dominance creates competitive barriers to entry.[29] At the same time, though, even if the combined airline is able to increase prices in some markets, the increase may be transitory if other airlines enter the markets with sufficient presence to counteract the price increase. In an empirical study of airline mergers and acquisitions up to 1992, Winston and Morrison suggest that being able to raise prices or stifle competition does not play a large role in airlines' merger and acquisition decisions.[30]

The other key financial benefit that airlines consider when merging with or acquiring another airline is the cost reduction that may result from combining complementary assets, eliminating duplicative activities, and reducing capacity. As we reported in May 2010, a merger or acquisition could enable the combined airline to reduce or eliminate duplicative operating costs, such as duplicative service, labor, and operations costs—including inefficient (or redundant) hubs or routes—or to achieve operational efficiencies by integrating computer systems and similar airline fleets.[31] By increasing the fleet size, airlines can increase their ability to match the size of aircraft with demand and adjust to seasonal shifts in demand. Other cost savings may stem from facility consolidation, procurement savings, and working capital and balance sheet restructuring, such as renegotiating aircraft leases. Airlines may also pursue mergers or acquisitions to more efficiently manage capacity—both to reduce operating costs and to generate revenue—in their networks. Given recent economic pressures, particularly increased fuel costs, the opportunity to lower costs by reducing redundant capacity may be especially appealing to airlines seeking to merge. In the case of the American–US Airways merger, airline executives estimate that the merger will allow $640 million in cost savings from reducing overlapping facilities at airports and in combining purchasing, technology, and corporate activities.

Table 1. Estimated Annual Benefits and Costs from American—US Airways Merger (Dollars in Billions)

Benefit	Estimated value
Revenue (network) benefit	$1.12
Cost benefits	.64
Increased labor costs	(.36)
Total annual benefits	$1.40

Source: US Airways.

Despite these benefits, there are several potential barriers to successfully consummating a merger, potentially reducing the benefits and increasing the costs. As we reported in July 2008,[32] the most significant operational challenges involve the integration of workforces, organizational cultures, aircraft fleets, and information technology systems and processes, challenges that can be difficult, disruptive, and costly as the airlines integrate.[33] For example, in the case of the American–US Airways merger, with unions supporting the merger, pilots' and others' pay will increase by $360 million annually if the merger is completed. However, merging workforces can take time–for example, US Airways' pilot seniority lists have not been resolved following their merger with America West in 2005. Integrating technology, especially reservation systems, can also be difficult and costly. For example, United has struggled to integrate computer and reservation systems following its merger with Continental in 2010.

THE PROPOSED AMERICAN AND US AIRWAYS MERGER WOULD CREATE THE LARGEST U.S. PASSENGER AIRLINE

If approved by DOJ, the merged American-US Airways would surpass United as the largest U.S. passenger airline. Table 2 shows that combining American and US Airways Airlines would create the largest U.S. airline based on data for the four quarters ending October 2012, as measured by capacity (available seat miles) and operating revenues. The combined airline would also have the largest workforce among U.S. airlines based on February 2013 employment statistics, with a combined 101,197 full-time equivalent employees (table 3). The airlines' workforces are represented by different unions, except dispatchers (table 4). Some of American's unions have already signed memorandums of understanding for future contracts if the airlines are merged. The combined airline would need to integrate 1,215 aircraft (table 5). American has a predominantly Boeing fleet, while US Airways has a largely Airbus fleet. In addition, in July 2011, American placed a $40 billion order for 200 Boeing 737 series and 260 Airbus A320 series aircraft. Despite its bankruptcy, the bankruptcy court allowed the order to proceed. American has also been trying to sell its regional airline, American Eagle, and its fleet of almost 280 aircraft.

If approved by DOJ, the airlines would combine two distinct networks supported by different hubs, where the airlines connect traffic feeding from smaller airports. American's major hubs are in Chicago O'Hare (ORD), Dallas (DFW), New York (JFK), Los Angeles (LAX), and Miami (MIA), and US

Airways has hubs in Charlotte (CLT), Philadelphia (PHL), Phoenix (PHX), and Washington D.C. (DCA), as shown in figures 4 and 5.

Table 2. Total Assets, Operating Revenue, and Capacity of Top U.S. Airlines (4 Quarters Ending October 2012)

Airline	Capacity as measured by available seat miles (thousands)	Total operating revenue (thousands)[a]	Total assets (thousands)
Combined American-US Airways	226,545,216	$38,847,509	$130,928,916
United	218,563,833	37,470,318	154,554,977
Delta	200,931,079	36,615,819	144,019,527
Southwest[b]	128,365,001	17,023,282	75,640,126
Alaska	27,655,088	4,561,605	19,770,760

Source: Bureau of Transportation Statistics Form 41.

[a] Revenues include revenues from regional operations but assets exclude regional carrier assets unless wholly owned, as in the case of American Eagle.

[b] Includes AirTran.

Table 3. Full-Time Equivalent Employees of Top U.S. Airlines (February 2013)

Full-Time Equivalent Employees	
Airline	Total
Combined American–US Airways[a]	101,197
United	82,212
Delta	73,320
Southwest	45,846
JetBlue	12,636
SkyWest	9,931
Alaska	9,279
Hawaiian	4,423

Source: Bureau of Transportation Statistics.

[a] Includes American Eagle.

Table 4. Union Representation for Various Employee Groups

	Employee groups			
	Pilots	Flight Attendants	Mechanics	Dispatchers
American	Allied Pilots Association (APA)	Association of Professional Flight Attendants (APFA)	Transport Workers Union (TWU)	TWU
US Airways	US Airline Pilots Association (USAPA)	Association of Flight Attendants (AFA)	International Association of Machinists and Aerospace Workers (IAM)	

Source: American Airlines and US Airways.

Table 5. American and US Airways Aircraft Fleet (2013)

Aircraft	American	US Airways	Merged
Embraer 190		18	18
Boeing 737	194	28	222
Boeing 757	104	24	128
Boeing 767	72	10	82
Boeing 777	49		49
Airbus 319		93	93
Airbus 320		72	72
Airbus321		75	75
Airbus 330		16	16
MD-80	188		188
CRJa	59		59
E135[a]	21		21
E140[a]	74		74
E145[a]	118		118
Total	879	336	1215

Source: American Airlines and Diio.

[a] American Eagle aircraft.

A key concern for DOJ in reviewing an airline merger is the loss of a competitor on nonstop routes. The loss of a competitor that serves a market on a nonstop basis is significant from a competitive perspective because nonstop service is typically preferred by most passengers and routes that only have nonstop service do not benefit from the availability of alternative, albeit lower valued, connecting service. Based on October 2012 traffic data, the two airlines overlap on 12 nonstop airport-pair routes, which are listed in figure 6.[34] For 7 of these 12 nonstop overlapping airport-pairs (generally between an American hub and a US Airways hub) there are currently no other competitors on a nonstop basis and in only one instance is a low cost airline (Southwest) present. And unlike the United—Continental merger, where most of the endpoint cities had other airports in the region, fewer of these airport pairs have significant other airports in the region. This is especially true for the Charlotte (CLT)—Dallas (DFW) and Phoenix (PHX)—DFW pairs where few alternate options are available at either endpoint.

The amount of overlap in airport-pair combinations is far more when considering all connecting traffic; however, on most of the overlapping airport-pair markets, there is at least one other competitor. Based on 2011 and 2012 ticket sample data, for 13,963 airport-pairs[35] with a minimum level of passenger traffic per year, there would be a loss of one effective competitor in 1,665 airport pair markets affecting more than 53 million passengers by merging these airlines (see figure 7).[36] As the figure shows, compared to the last major airline merger in 2010 between United and Continental, there would be 530 more airport pairs losing an effective competitor. This would affect 18 million more passengers compared to the merger between United and Continental. In addition, any effect on fares may be dampened by the presence of a low cost airline in 473 of the 1,665 airport pairs losing a competitor.[37] The combination of the two airlines would also create a new effective competitor with at least a combined 5 percent market share in 210 airport-pairs affecting 17.5 million passengers.

If approved by DOJ, the combined airline could be expected to rationalize its network over time, including where it maintains hubs. The two airlines do not share any airport hubs; therefore, the amount of airport market share overlap that currently exists at these hubs is relatively small but could grow at some hubs while contracting at others under a merger (see table 6). For example, New York could serve as a better hub and international gateway than Philadelphia in the Northeast, while Miami could be a better hub than Charlotte in the Southeast. In addition, 59 out of 116 domestic airports served by US Airways from Charlotte are also served by American from Miami (MIA). Closing hubs is not unprecedented, following the American acquisition of TWA in 2001, St Louis ceased to be an American hub and following the Delta–Northwest merger, service at Delta's hub in Cincinnati and Northwest's hub in Memphis has been greatly reduced.

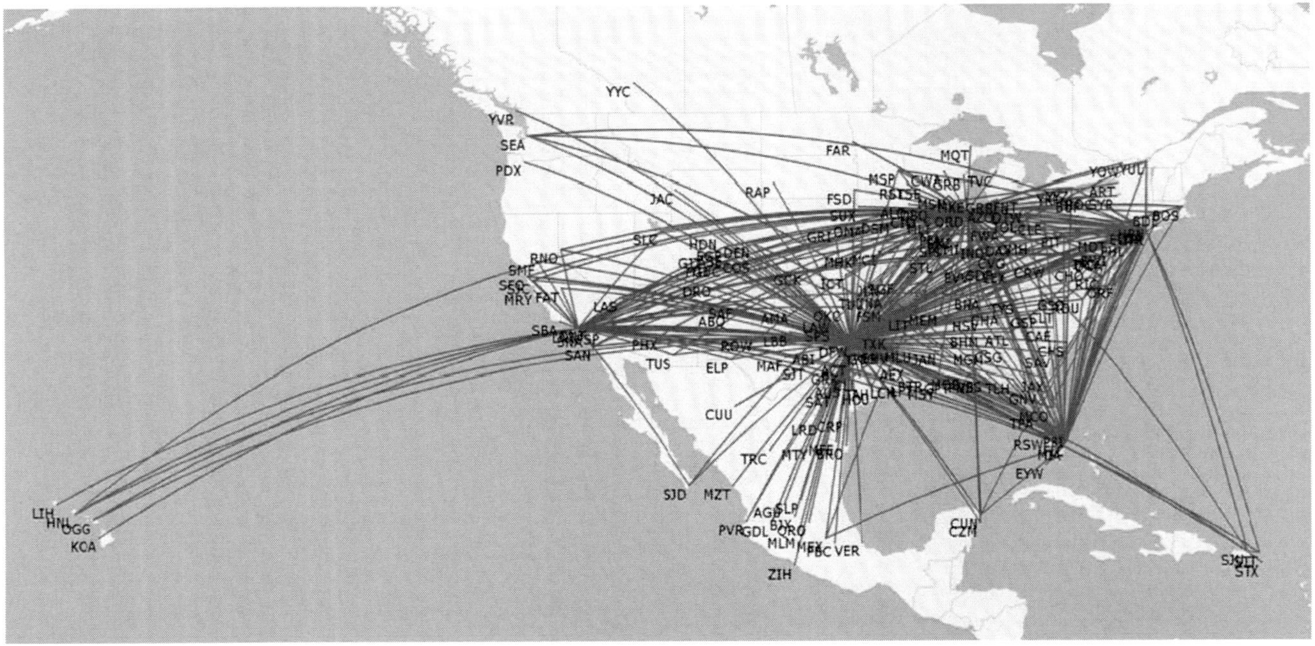

Source: Innovata schedule data.

Figure 4. American Airlines Domestic Route Maps (January 2013).

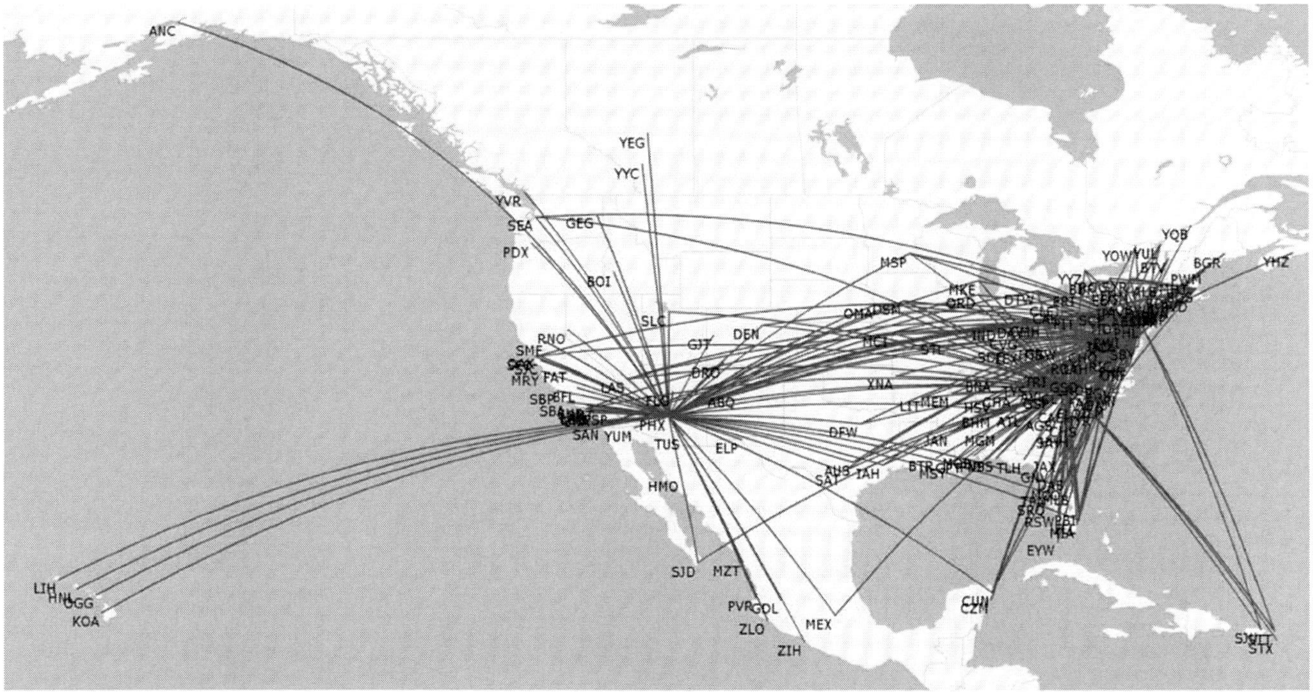

Source: Innovata schedule data.

Figure 5. US Airways Domestic Route Maps (January 2013).

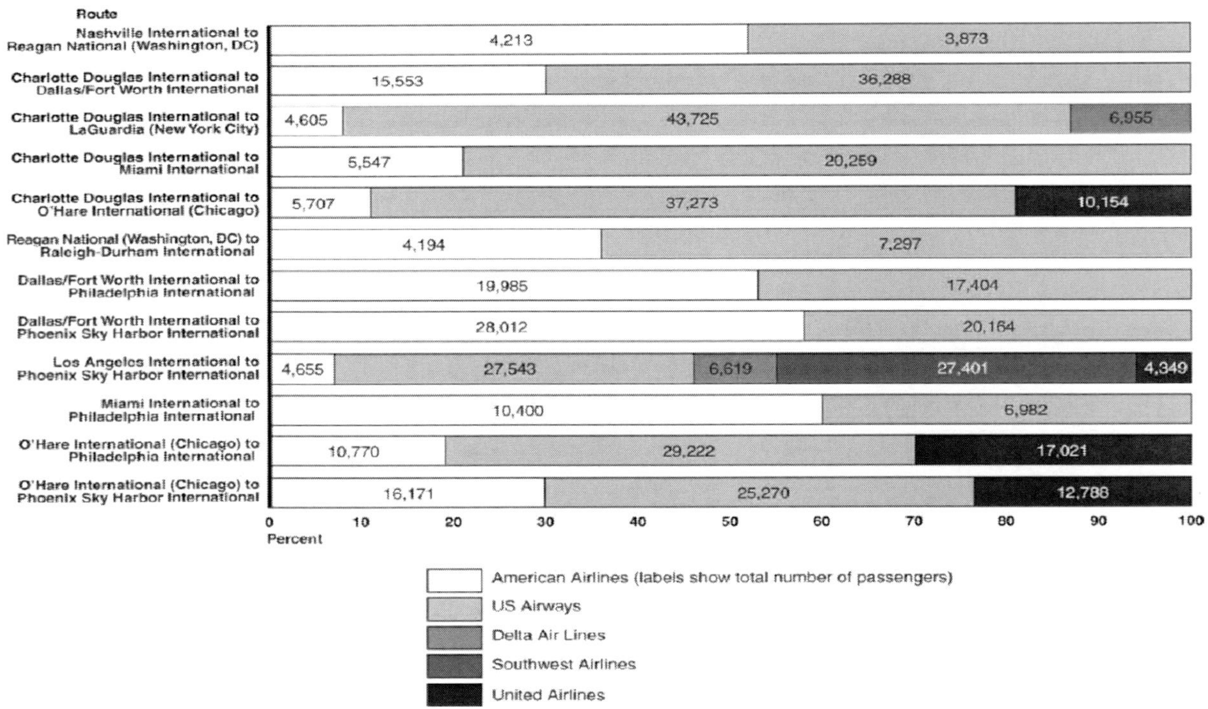

Source: GAO analysis of DOT T-100 traffic data.

Figure 6. Total Passengers on Overlapping Nonstop Airport Pairs (October 2012).

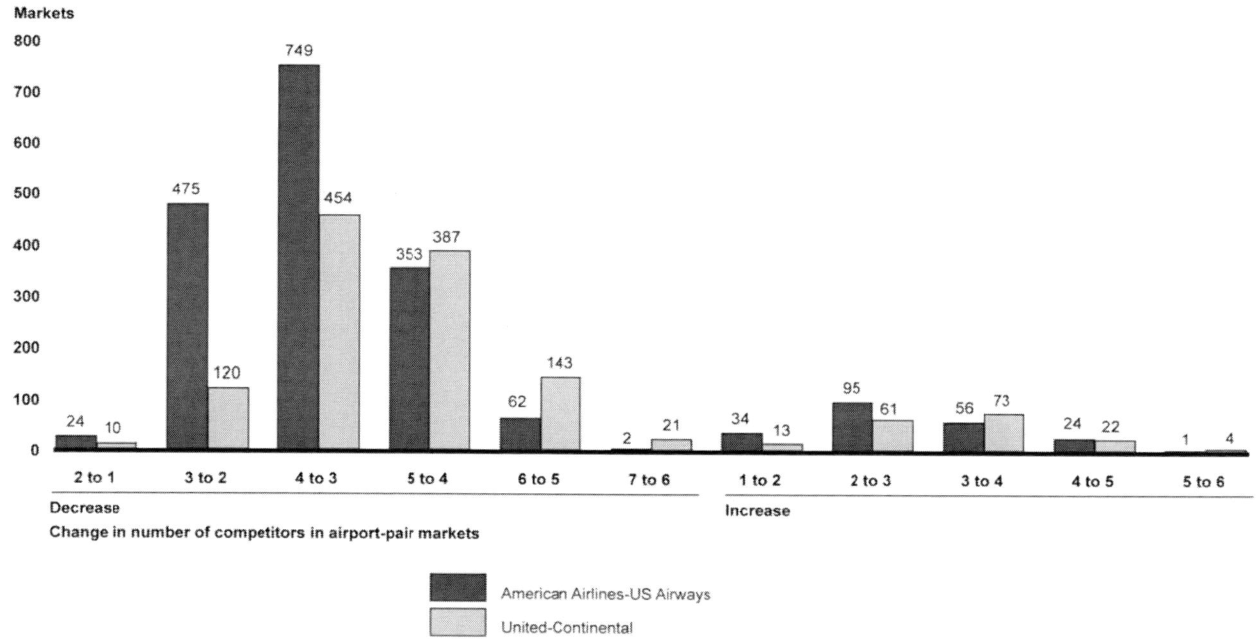

Source: GAO analysis of DOT Origin & Destination (OD1B) ticket data.

Note: All origin and destination airport pairs with at least 520 passengers in either direction. An effective competitor holds at least 5 percent of market share.

Figure 7. Change in Effective Competition from American-US Airways Combination (2012) Compared to United-Continental Merger (2010).

Table 6. Domestic Passenger Market Share at Hub and Key Airports (4 Quarters Ending October 2012)

American airports	American share (%)	US Airways airports	US Airways share (%)	Total (%)
Dallas (DFW)	67		7	74
Miami (MIA)	66		6	72
	7	**Charlotte (CLT)**	63	70
	5	**Philadelphia (PHL)**	49	54
	15	**Washington DC (DCA)**	34	49
Chicago (ORD)	36		7	43
New York (LGA)	20		14	34
	5	**Phoenix (PHX)**	27	32
Los Angeles (LAX)	18		5	23
New York (JFK)	15		3	18

Source: DOT origin and destination ticket sample data.
Note: Hub airports in bold.

Table 7. Slot Holdings of American and US Airways at Slot-Controlled Airports (February 2012)

Airports	American share (%)	US Airways share (%)	Combined American – US share (%)	United share (%)	Delta share (%)	Other share (%)
Washington DC (DCA)	14	54	68	9	12	11
New York LaGuardia (LGA)	22	11	33	5	46	16
New York (JFK)	18	1	19	4	40	36
Newark (EWR)	5	3	8	81	6	6

Source: FAA.

Three of the airports noted in table 6 are slot-controlled airports with restricted access for new entrants or expanded service. As we reported last year, slot-controlled airports have more limited competition and tend to have higher fares compared to other hub airports.[38] Based on February 2012 slot holdings, a combined American and US Airways would control one-third of the slots at LaGuardia and two-thirds of the slots at Washington Reagan as noted in Table 7.

Both American and US Airways have worldwide networks and serve many international destinations. Between the two airlines, they serve 107 international cities from airports in the United States, 37 of them in common, according to published February 2013 schedules. However, the two airlines do not directly compete on any of the same international city pair markets, though both serve slot-controlled London Heathrow airport with more than 830,000 passengers over the last year.[39] For international routes, U.S. airlines aggregate traffic from many domestic locations at a hub airport where passengers transfer onto international flights. In other words, at Philadelphia, where US Airways has a large hub, passengers traveling from many locations across the U.S. transfer onto US Airways' international flights. Likewise, American aggregates domestic traffic at New York's JFK for many of its international flights to some of the same destinations. As such, a passenger traveling from, for example Nashville, may view these alternative routes to a location in Europe as substitutable.

Whether service to international destinations from different domestic hubs will be viewed as a competitive concern will likely depend on a host of factors, such as the two airlines' market share of traffic to that destination and whether there are any barriers to new airlines entering or existing airlines expanding service at the international destination airports. US Airways is part of the larger Star Alliance, and American is a member of the smaller oneworld alliance. [40] US Airways has announced it will leave the Star Alliance and join American in oneworld as part of the merger. The DOT has authority to approve antitrust immunity applications,[41] but DOJ may also comment if it has antitrust concerns. According to a 2011 paper prepared by DOJ economists, "Over the past 17 years, DOT granted immunity to over 20 international alliance agreements, permitting participants in these alliances to collude on prices, schedules, and marketing."[42] They found that in granting immunity to larger groups of airlines in the three major international alliances, the number of independent competitors over the North Atlantic was significantly reduced adversely affecting consumers through higher fares. Because both airlines are already part of immunized alliances it is unclear what effect, if any, this merger might have on competition in international service. According to DOT officials responsible for reviewing and approving the immunity requests, the agency has analyzed and documented the impact of immunized alliances in its many public orders and has concluded that in its experience, integrated airline alliances enable a number of valuable consumer benefits, including lower prices for many travelers.

Chairman Cantwell, Ranking Member Ayotte, and Members of the Subcommittee, this concludes my prepared statement. I would be happy to answer any questions that you may have at this time.

End Notes

[1] Pub. L. No. 95-504, 92 Stat. 1705 (1978).

[2] See list of related GAO products attached to this statement.

[3] Under the Hart-Scott-Rodino Act, an acquisition of voting securities and/or assets above a set monetary amount must be reported to DOJ (or the Federal Trade Commission for certain industries) so the department can determine whether the merger or acquisition poses any antitrust concerns. 15 U.S.C. § 18a(d)(1). Both DOJ and the Federal Trade Commission have antitrust enforcement authority, including reviewing proposed mergers and acquisitions. DOJ is the antitrust enforcement authority charged with reviewing proposed mergers and acquisitions in the airline industry.

[4] GAO, *Airline Mergers: Issues Raised by the Proposed Merger of United and Continental Airlines,* GAO-10-778T (Washington, D.C., May 27, 2010).

[5] GAO, *Airline Industry: Potential Mergers and Acquisitions Driven by Financial and Competitive Pressures*, GAO-08-845 (Washington, D.C.: July 31, 2008).

[6] *Commercial Aviation: Airline Industry Contraction Due to Volatile Fuel Prices and Falling Demand Affects Airports, Passengers, and Federal Government Revenues,* GAO-09-393 (Washington, D.C.: Apr. 21, 2009) and GAO-08-845.

[7] Civil Aeronautics Board Sunset Act, Pub. L. No. 98-443, 98 Stat. 1703 (1984).

[8] GAO, *Aviation Competition: Issues Related to the Proposed United Airlines-US Airways Merger*, GAO-01-212 (Washington, D.C.: Dec. 15, 2000) p. 10, footnote 6.

[9] PBGC was established under the Employee Retirement Income Security Act of 1974 (Pub. L. No. 93-406, 88 Stat. 1003 (1974) (ERISA) and set forth standards and requirements that apply to defined benefit plans. PBGC was established to encourage the continuation and maintenance of voluntary private pension plans and to insure the benefits of workers and retirees in defined benefit plans should plan sponsors fail to pay benefits. PGBC operations are financed, for example, by insurance premiums paid by sponsors of defined benefit plans, investment income, and assets from pension plans trusted by PBGC, and recoveries from the companies formerly responsible for the plans.

[10] The six airlines receiving loan guarantees were Aloha, World, Frontier, US Airways, ATA, and America West.

[11] GAO, *Commercial Aviation: Bankruptcy and Pensions Problems Are Symptoms of Underlying Structural Issues*, GAO-05-945 (Washington, D.C.: Sept. 30, 2005).

[12] Network (or legacy) airlines are essentially those airlines that were in operation before the Airline Deregulation Act of 1978 and whose goal is to provide service from "anywhere to everywhere." To meet that goal, these airlines support large, complex hub-and-spoke operations with thousands of employees and with hundreds of aircraft of various types, with service at numerous fare levels to domestic communities of all sizes and to international destinations. For purposes of this report, we have defined American, Continental, Delta, Northwest, United, and US Airways as network airlines and Allegiant, AirTran, Frontier, Midwest, JetBlue, Southwest, Spirit, and Sun Country as low cost airlines.

[13] Randall Bennett and James Craun, U.S. Department of Transportation, *The Airline Deregulation Evolution Continues: The Southwest Effect*, May 1993.

[14] Austan Goolsbee and Chad Syverson, "How Do Incumbents Respond to the Threat of Entry? Evidence from the Major Airlines," *The Quarterly Journal of Economics*, (November 2008).

[15] Najmus Sakib bin Salam, *Is There Still A Southwest Effect?* Transportation Research Record publications, Volume no. 2325 (May 2013).

[16] The *Guidelines* were jointly developed by DOJ's Antitrust Division and the Federal Trade Commission (FTC) and describe the inquiry process the two agencies follow in analyzing proposed mergers. The current version of the *Guidelines* was revised in August 2010.

[17] 49 USC § 41110.

[18] Pub. L. No. 94-435, 90 Stat. 1383 (1976).

[19] See 15 U.S.C. § 18a(d)(1). Under the Hart-Scott-Rodino Act, DOJ has 30 days after the initial filing to notify companies that intend to merge whether DOJ requires additional information for its review. If DOJ does not request additional information, the firms can close their deal (15 U.S.C. § 18a(b)). If more information is required, however, the initial 30-day waiting period is followed by a second 30-day period, which starts to run after both companies have provided the requested information (15 USC § 18a(e)(2)). Companies often attempt to resolve DOJ competitive concerns, if possible, prior to the expiration of the second waiting period. Any restructuring of a transaction—e.g., through a divestiture— is included in a consent decree entered by a court, unless the competitive problem is unilaterally fixed by the parties prior to the expiration of the waiting period (called a "fix-it first").

[20] "Market power" is the ability to maintain prices profitably above competitive levels for a significant period of time.

[21] United States Department of Justice and Federal Trade Commission, *Horizontal Merger Guidelines* (Washington, D.C., rev. Aug. 19, 2010).

[22] 49 U.S.C. § 41104.

[23] 49 U.S.C. § 44702.

[24] 49 U.S.C. § 41105. DOT must specifically consider the "transfer-of-certificate" authority's impact on the financial viability of the parties to the transaction and on the trade position of the United States in the international air transportation market, as well as on competition in the domestic airline industry.

[25] 11 U.S.C. § 1101 et seq. Chapter 11 of the United States code governs business reorganizations. This chapter is designed to accommodate complicated reorganizations of publicly held corporations. Among other things, it allows companies, with court approval, to reject agreements made under collective bargaining and renegotiate contracts with other creditors. With the approval of the bankruptcy courts (which administer the bankruptcy laws), companies may also modify retiree benefits.

[26] On April 15, American filed a formal restructuring plan to exit bankruptcy protection based on its merger with US Airways. On May10, 2013, the presiding judge in the American Airlines bankruptcy signed an order approving the merger between American Airlines and US Airways. *In re AMR Corp.,* United States Bankruptcy Court for the Southern District of New York, No. 11-15463-SHL.

[27] GAO-10-778T.

[28] See Severin Borenstein, "Airline Mergers, Airport Dominance, and Market Power," *American Economic Review*, Vol. 80 (May 1990); Steven A. Morrison, "Airline Mergers: A Longer View," *Journal of Transport Economics and Policy* (September 1996); and Gregory J. Werden, Andrew J. Joskow, and Richard L. Johnson, "The Effects of Mergers on Price and Output: Two Case Studies from the Airline Industry," *Managerial and Decision Economics*, Vol. 12 (October 1991).

[29] See Severin Borenstein, "Hubs and High Fares: Dominance and Market Power in the U.S. Airline Industry," *RAND Journal of Economics*, 20, 344-365 (1989); GAO, *Airline Deregulation: Barriers to Entry Continue to Limit Competition in Several Key Markets*,

GAO/RCED-97-4 (Washington, D.C.: Oct. 18, 1996); and GAO, *Airline Competition: Effects of Airline and Market Concentration and Barriers to Entry on Airfares*, GAO/RCED-91-101 (Washington, D.C.: Apr. 16, 1991).

[30] See Steven A. Morrison, and Clifford Winston, "The Remaining Role for Government Policy in the Deregulated Airline Industry." *Deregulation of Network Industries: What's Next? eds.* Sam Peltzman and Clifford Winston, (Washington, D.C., Brookings Institution Press 2000) pp. 1-40.

[31] GAO-10-778T.

[32] GAO-08-845.

[33] Airlines also face potential challenges to mergers and acquisitions from DOJ's antitrust review, which is discussed in the previous section.

[34] This compares coincidently to the same number of nonstop overlapping airport pairs in the United—Continental merger.

[35] It is generally preferable, time permitting, to assess city-pair, rather than airport-pair, changes in competition. Some larger U.S. cities (New York, Chicago, Los Angeles, Washington, D.C.) have more than one commercial airport that can compete for passenger traffic. DOJ generally considers the relevant market to be a city-pair combination, but also examines the airport pair if relevant.

[36] We assessed more than 96,000 airport pairs with any passenger traffic over the last 4 quarters ending October 2012, but eliminated any airport-pair with 520 or fewer annual passengers in one direction or 1,040 for two-way traffic because they would to be too small to ensure statistical accuracy. We defined an effective competitor as having at least 5 percent of total airport pair traffic. These are the same minimum passenger and market share that we have previously used to assess whether an airline has sufficient presence in a market to affect competition. See GAO-10-778T and GAO-08-845.

[37] We defined low cost airlines as JetBlue, Frontier/Midwest, AirTran, Allegiant, Spirit, Sun Country, and Southwest.

[38] GAO, *Slot-Controlled Airports: FAA's Rules Could be Improved to Enhance Competition and Use of Available Capacity,* GAO-12-902 (Washington, D.C., Sept. 13, 2012).

[39] Of these 830,000 passengers, US Airways transported 52,000 and American Airlines transported 778,000.

[40] An airline alliance is an agreement between two or more airlines to cooperate on a substantial level. The three largest passenger airline alliances are the Star Alliance, SkyTeam and oneworld. Alliances provide a network of connectivity and convenience for international passengers. Alliances also provide convenient marketing branding to facilitate travelers making inter airline "codeshare" connections within countries.

[41] 49 U.S.C. §§ 41308, 41309.

[42] See William Gillespie and Oliver Richard, "Antitrust Immunity and International Airline Alliances", *Economic Analysis Group of the Department of Justice's Antitrust Division,* EAG 11-1, February 2011. The views are those of the authors and not the department.

In: Airline Competition and Consolidation ISBN: 978-1-63463-119-8
Editor: Caroline Reid

Chapter 3

REDUCTIONS IN COMPETITION INCREASE AIRLINE FLIGHT DELAYS AND CANCELLATIONS*

U.S. Department of Transportation, Office of Inspector General

MEMORANDUM

Date: April 23, 2014

Subject: *Action*: Reductions in Competition Increase Airline Flight Delays and Cancellations Federal Aviation Administration
Report No. CR-2014-040

From: Mitchell Behm
Assistant Inspector General for Surface
Transportation Audits[1]

To: Federal Aviation Administrator

---

* This is an edited, reformatted and augmented version of an audit report, CR-2014-040, issued by the U.S. Department of Transportation, April 23, 2014.

Since 2005, the U.S. airline industry's service quality—airlines' on-time performance and cancellation rates—has varied greatly. The percentage of late domestic flights has fluctuated between 11 and 33 percent per month, while the rate of cancellations has varied from under 1 percent to over 5 percent per month. Understanding the sources of these variations is important because airline delays and cancellations have affected a large number of flights. For example, 1 percent of domestic flights equaled 60,968 flights in 2012.[2]

There has also been considerable industry consolidation since 2005 with mergers between Delta and Northwest in 2008, United and Continental in 2010, and American and US Airways in late 2013. Public concerns over a possible relationship between the quality of airline service and industry consolidation led to congressional hearings and requests to the accountability community to review these issues.[3] Section 406 of the FAA Modernization and Reform Act of 2012 required our office to assess the effects of limited airline service options on the frequency of delays and cancellations.[4] This report presents the results of our analyses of the relationship between competition, measured at the individual route level, and airline service quality, also measured at the individual route level.

Our objective was to determine whether limited competition affects flight delays and cancellations. Specifically, we determined whether (1) reductions in competition affected the percentage of late flights and the length of flight delays, (2) reductions in competition affected flight cancellation rates, and (3) the effects of reduced competition on airline service quality depended upon the initial level of competition.

We conducted our audit work from October 2012 through March 2014, in accordance with generally accepted Government auditing standards. To conduct our work, we collected data on 2,530 domestic routes[5] flown by 20 airlines[6] from the fourth quarter of calendar year 2005 through the fourth quarter of calendar year 2012. We then constructed econometric models to estimate the effect of competition on the length of arrival delay, the percentage of total flights that were late, and the percentage of total flights that were cancelled. For additional information on our scope and methodology, see exhibit A.

RESULTS IN BRIEF

Our study found that variation in airline service quality related substantially to changes in the level of competition within airline markets.

Specifically, when airline markets became less competitive both the average length of flight delays and percentage of late flights increased. The effects of reduced competition on the average length of flight delay were statistically significant and sizeable. We estimated that when a market's service options shrank from three airlines to two,[7] the length of delays in the market increased by 25.3 percent. However, the impact of reduced competition on the percentage of late flights was only minimally statistically significant and small in size.

We also found that when competition declined, cancellation rates increased to an extent that was both highly statistically significant and substantial in size. We estimated that a market that went from being served by three airlines to two experienced nearly a 7 percent increase in the flight cancellation rate due to the loss of competition.

Finally, we found that the degree to which competition affected delay lengths and cancellations depended on initial levels of market competition.[8] We estimated that when a market started out fairly competitive, reduced competition significantly increased the lengths of delays but did not substantially affect delay lengths in a market that started out with little initial competition. Conversely, following a similar reduction in competition, we estimated that passengers in markets initially served by few airlines experienced a greater increase in the cancellation rate than passengers in markets initially served by many airlines.

BACKGROUND

We performed both descriptive and statistical modeling analyses to examine the relationship between service quality and market competition. These two types of analyses differed as follows.

- **Descriptive analyses** – These analyses took into account the level of competition but could not separate its effects from those of other factors, such as weather and labor disputes, which could also affect service quality.
- **Statistical analyses** – These analyses isolated the effects of competition on delays and cancellation rates from the effects of other factors affecting airline service quality—such as weather and congestion—and tested them for statistical significance.[9]

We constructed a sample of over 32.2 million flights with flight performance information from 70 U.S. airports.[10] We used this sample to construct econometric models of airline performance. Our modeling served as the basis for our statistical analyses, allowing us to control for factors other than the level of competition that likely affect airline service quality.[11] We constructed separate models for three service quality measures: average minutes of arrival delay;[12] percentage of total flights that were late;[13] and percentage of total flights that were cancelled.

We measured competition by constructing a Hirschman-Herfindahl index (HHI), a commonly used measure of market competition based on the distribution of market revenue shares. An HHI ranges from 0 to 1. The index approaches zero when a market is served by a large number of airlines of relatively equal size and reaches one when a market is controlled by a single airline. The index increases both as the number of airlines in a market decreases and as disparity in the size of those airlines increases.

We defined an airline market as a pair of origin and destination airports. The definition includes direct flights[14] and flights requiring one connection, since flights with one connection are often considered reasonable substitutes for direct flights. The definition covers more than 95 percent of the passengers[15] during the sample period. We generated an alternative measure of market competition based only on direct flights for use in checking the robustness of our results.

Based on our measure of the level of competitiveness, we characterize the U.S. domestic airline industry as concentrated, with most markets dominated by two carriers. Thirteen percent of the routes in our sample were monopoly routes dominated by one carrier (HHI of 0.9 to 1.0). Forty-two percent were concentrated routes dominated by two carriers (HHI of 0.5 to 0.9). We categorized the rest of the markets (44 percent) as competitive routes (HHI of 0.0 to 0.5).[16] Even though we considered these routes competitive, the competitiveness was relative because, even though there were more than two carriers, many of these routes were dominated by only three airlines.

DELAYS INCREASED WHEN COMPETITION DECREASED

When competition decreased, both the average length of flight delays and percentage of total flights that were late increased. The relationship of reduced competition to increases in the average length of flight delays was substantial and statistically significant. There is less statistical support to infer that reduced competition increased the percentage of late flights.

The Average Length of Flight Delays Increased with Reduced Competition

The average length of flight delays on a route increased as the amount of competition decreased. In our descriptive analyses, we plotted the average length of delay in our sample at each level of our measure of competition. The relationship was most apparent where competition was highest (HHI of 0.1 to 0.3). Across lower levels of competition (HHI of 0.3 to 1.0), there was no apparent relationship between competition and the delay length. See figure 1 for details.

Our statistical analyses revealed that the relationship between competition and average minutes of delay was highly statistically significant,[17] and the impact of competition on delay length was sizeable. For example, in our sample, a passenger in a market served by three airlines experienced, on average, a delay of 4 minutes and 40 seconds. However, we estimated that when the number of airlines serving a market decreased from three airlines to two, the reduction in competition increased that average delay by 1 minute and 11 seconds, or 25.3 percent (see figure 2).

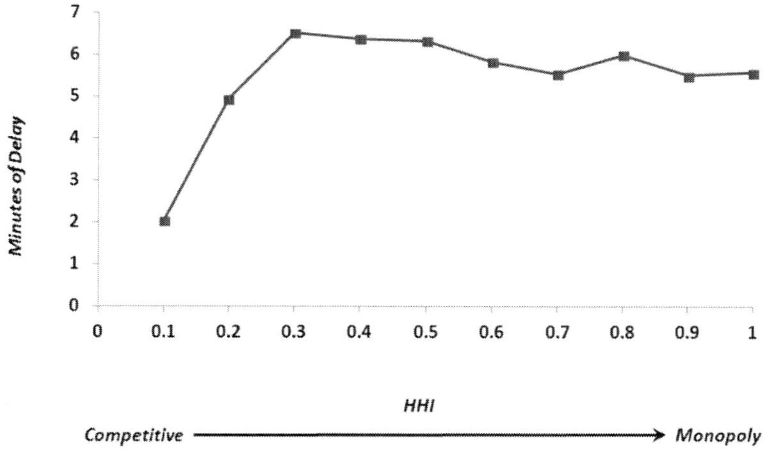

Source: OIG descriptive analysis.

Figure 1. Competition and Average Minutes of Delay.

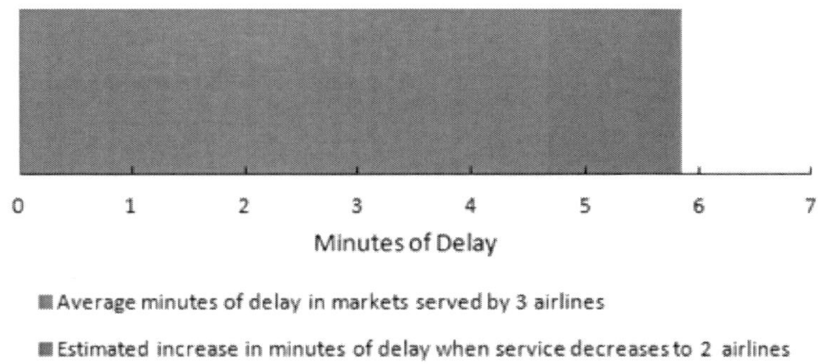

Source: OIG statistical analysis

Figure 2. The Impact of Reduced Competition on Delay Length[18].

There Was Little Evidence of a Link between Competition and the Frequency of Late Flights

There was little evidence of a link between competition and the frequency of late flights. In our descriptive analysis, we plotted airline competition against the percentage of total flights, and found that the results did not show a strong relationship (see figure 3). The percentage of total flights that were late increased slightly when the competition index was low (HHI from 0.1 to 0.3), only to decrease later (HHI from 0.3 to 1.0).

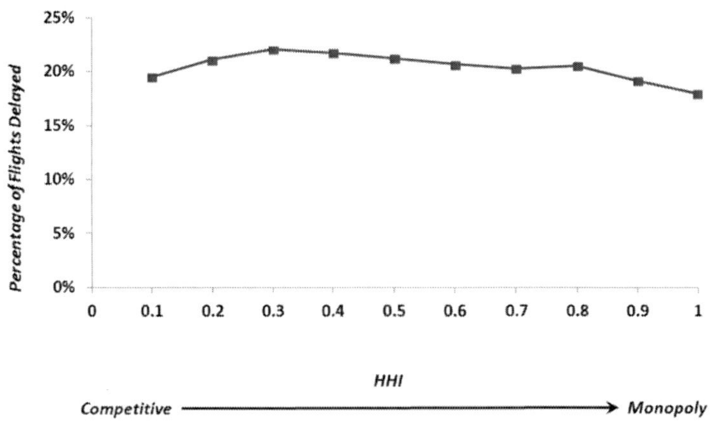

Source: OIG descriptive analysis.

Figure 3. Competition and the Percentage of Late Flights.

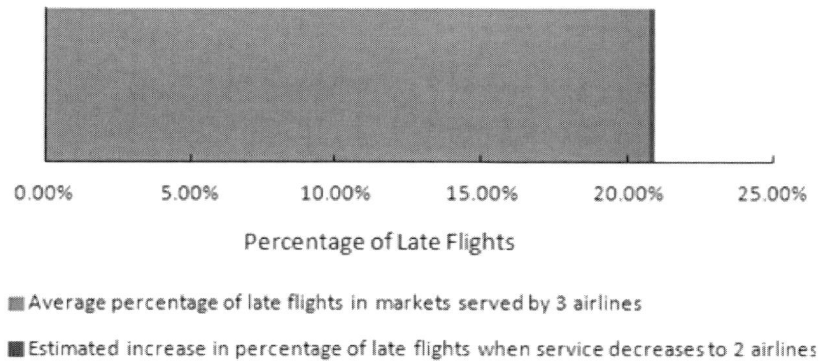

Source: OIG statistical analysis.

Figure 4. The Impact of Reduced Competition on Percentage of Late Flights.

According to our statistical analysis, the percentage of late flights increased when competition decreased. However, this relationship was only minimally statistically significant.[19] Furthermore, the effect of a reduction in competition was minor. For example, the average percentage of flights that were late in markets served by 3 airlines was 20.78 percent. When service was reduced to two airlines, we estimated that the average frequency of late flights increased to 20.91 percent— less than 1 percent (see figure 4).

The Percentage of Cancelled Flights Increased as Competition Decreased

When route competition fell, cancellation rates increased. The descriptive analysis graph (see figure 5) indicated that the overall cancellation rate increased as competition decreased, even though for part of the graph—from an HHI of 0.4 to 0.9—airline competition and cancellations appeared to have no relationship.

According to our statistical analysis, the impact of competition on cancellation rates was large and highly statistically significant.[20] For example, markets served by three airlines experienced average cancellation rates of 1.46 percent. We estimated the cancellation rates in markets with reductions in service from three airlines to two reached 1.56 percent—close to a 7 percent increase—due to the loss of competition (see figure 6).[21]

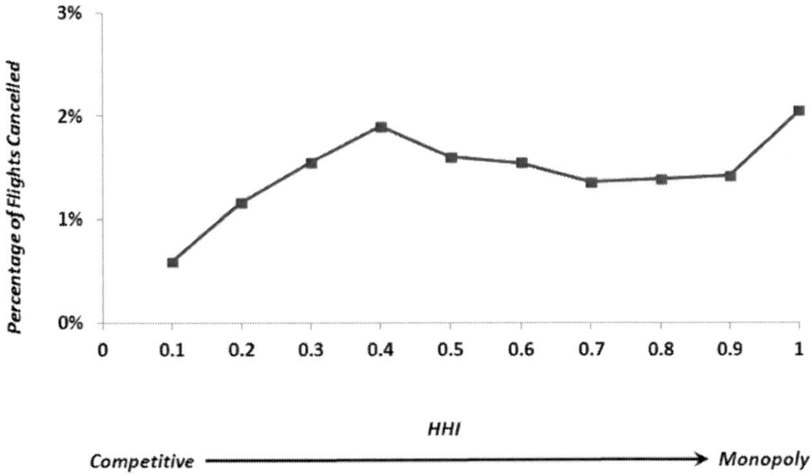

Source: OIG descriptive analysis.

Figure 5. Competition and the Cancellation Rate.

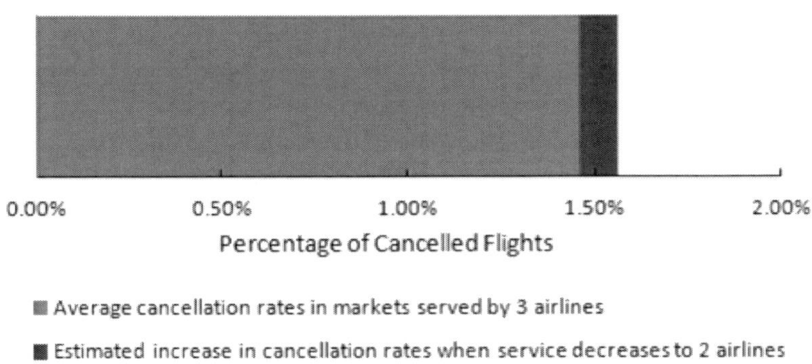

Source: OIG statistical analysis.

Figure 6. The Impact of Reduced Competition on Cancellation Rates.

EFFECTS OF REDUCED COMPETITION ON AIRLINE SERVICE QUALITY DEPENDED ON INITIAL COMPETITION LEVELS[22]

The degree to which reduced competition affected delay lengths and cancellation rates depended on initial competition levels. We estimated that reduced competition had a marked increase on lengths of delays in a market initially served by many airlines but did not substantially affect delays in markets that started out with a low level of competition. Conversely, we estimated that when a market started with a high level of competition, a reduction in competition did not substantially increase the rate of flight cancellations but did increase them in markets with initially limited service options.

The Largest Increases in Average Delay Lengths Occurred in Markets with Reductions in Initially High Levels of Competition

When a market was initially served by several carriers, we estimated that lengths of delays increased substantially with reduced competition. However, we also estimated that subsequent reductions in competition had less impact. For example, we estimated that when the number of airlines serving a market went from three to two, the market experienced a 25.3 percent increase in average minutes of delay. The increase experienced in a market that went from two airlines to one was not much larger, 26.5 percent, even though the latter change represents a substantially larger competition reduction as measured by the HHI–0.500 versus 0.167.[23] As illustrated in figure 7, when the HHI increased by 0.1, the estimated effect on a market's average minutes of delay varies from approximately 61 seconds to as little as 5 seconds, with the smaller impacts associated with the less competitive markets.

The Largest Increases in Flight Cancellation Rates Occurred in Markets with Little Initial Competition

In a market with many airlines, we estimated that reduced competition had less impact on the percentage of total cancelled flights than a similar reduction in a market with little initial competition. For example, as seen in figure 8, we estimated that a 0.1 increase in the HHI was associated with increments to the cancellation rate from .053 to .069 percent, with the larger increases associated with the less competitive markets. Consequently, we estimated that the largest increase in cancellation rates occurred in markets that became monopolies.

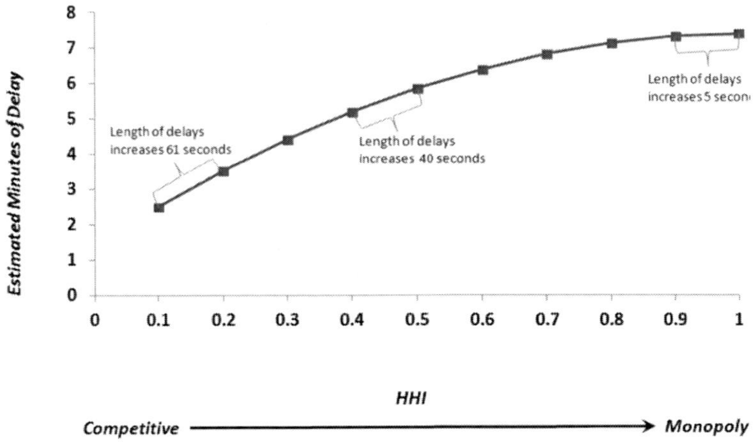

Source: OIG statistical analysis.

Figure 7. Estimated Relationship Between Competition and Minutes of Delay.

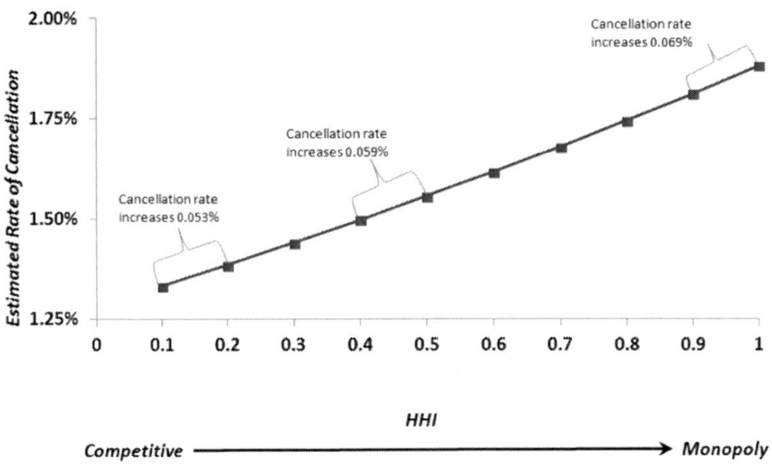

Source: OIG statistical analysis.

Figure 8. Estimated Relationship Between Competition and Cancellation Rates.

CONCLUDING OBSERVATIONS

Through our statistical analysis, we determined that variation in airline service quality related substantially to changes in the level of competition within airline markets. Specifically, reduced airline competition increased both the length of delays in some markets and the number of flight cancellations in others. Further, passengers in historically competitive markets experienced a substantial increase in the length of flight delays as competition declined. On the other hand, passengers in historically less competitive markets experienced a larger increase in cancellation rates following a reduction in competition. This type of economic analysis serves to inform FAA and the Department of Transportation about the impacts of reduced competition on airline service quality, and can be used as information in future planning to advance an efficient air traffic system for the traveling public.

Agency Comments and Office of Inspector General Response

On March 20, 2014, we provided copies of this draft report to FAA and the Office of the Secretary. Both informed us that they had no comments on this independent analysis. No actions are required.

We appreciate the courtesies and cooperation of Department of Transportation representatives during this audit. If you have any questions concerning this report, please call me at (202) 366-9970, or Betty Krier, Program Director, at (202) 366-1422.

cc: Assistant Secretary for Aviation and International Affairs
FAA Deputy Administrator
DOT Audit Liaison, M1
FAA Audit Liaison, AAE-100

Exhibit A. Scope and Methodology

We conducted our work from October 2012 through March 2014, in accordance with generally accepted Government auditing standards. Those standards require that we plan and perform the audit to obtain sufficient, appropriate evidence to provide a reasonable basis for our findings and conclusions based on our audit objectives. We believe that the evidence obtained provides a reasonable basis for our findings based on our audit objectives.

The FAA Modernization and Reform Act of 2012 directed our office to assess the effect that limited air carrier service options have on the frequency of delays and cancellations. Our audit objective was to determine whether limited competition has substantially affected flight delays and cancellations. We defined competition using a standard index based on airlines' market shares. We defined substantially affect as having a statistically and economically significant impact.

To conduct our work, we performed an econometric analysis using airline data on 2,530 domestic directional airport-pairs from the fourth quarter of 2005 through the fourth quarter of 2012. Our sample contained 20 airlines, 15 of which were major carriers.[24] The Bureau of Transportation Statistics (BTS) defines a major carrier as one with annual revenues in excess of $1 billion. The remaining airlines were national carriers,[25] which BTS defines as having annual revenues between $100 million and $1 billion.

We began construction of our sample by combining the on-time performance data from the Airline Service Quality Performance (ASQP) database and the Data and Airline Origin and Destination survey (DB1B) information, both of which BTS maintains. DB1B is a quarterly 10 percent sample of all airline tickets issued by reporting carriers.[26] We measured competition by constructing HHIs based on data from DB1B. We defined an airline market as a directional origin and destination airport-pair. We used BTS's Air Carrier Statistics Database (T-100) to identify service type. The T-100 data also included data on aircraft characteristics and load factors, defined as the monthly average ratio of total passengers and seats. We used weather data from the National Climatic Data Center. We obtained airport capacity utilization data from the FAA's Aviation Performance Metrics (APM) Airport Efficiency System.[27]

To ensure sufficient time series variation for statistical estimation, we omitted route-carrier groups with data spanning less than one year. We also excluded observations with either an origin or destination outside the continental U.S. and flights that arrived more than one hour early or six hours late. We excluded any route that reported less than eight flights per month. The sample was substantially reduced after merging with airport capacity utilization data, because that data is only available for 77 large airports, and only 73 of these are within the continental U.S. With 2,530 directional airport-pairs, 5,481 route-carrier combinations, and 298,389 monthly observations (298,523 for our cancellation analyses), our final sample encompassed approximately 71 percent of the total number of flights during the sample period in the ASQP database.[28]

We built three econometric models to investigate the effect of airline competition on flight delays and cancellations. The dependent variables, or measures whose variation we were seeking to explain, were minutes of arrival delays, percentage of late flights, and percentage of cancelled flights. We also developed a list of factors, or control variables, to account or control for variation in the airline service measures that was not associated with the degree of competition. We developed the list of control variables in part from interviews with the vice president/chief economist at Airlines for America and an independent airline expert. We also drew from economics literature on factors significantly affecting airline service quality. The list of control variables was the same for all three models.

We categorized our control variables into weather factors (heavy rain and freezing rain), profitability measure (load factor), and route-carrier specific covariates. Examples of route-carrier controls included monthly departures in various time windows, congestion measures, and aircraft types. Our congestion measures were unique because they were route-carrier specific based on our construction and accessibility to FAA airport capacity utilization data. The variable of focus was the competition measure, which was an HHI generated with airlines' shares of market revenues. To check the robustness of our findings, we also measured competition using shares of market passengers. The results changed very little with this alternative definition. Sensitivity analyses are detailed in Exhibit B.

EXHIBIT B. DETAILED SCOPE AND METHODOLOGY

This exhibit describes our scope and methodology in technical detail. It is organized as follows. First, we describe the sources, construction, and characteristics of our estimation sample. Second, we detail our model specifications and estimation approaches. The last section discusses our results and sensitivity analyses.

Data Sources and the Estimation Sample

We constructed our sample using various data sources. All data was converted into monthly averages and covered the period of 2005:4Q-2012:4Q. Flight delay, measured by minutes of arrival delay, and cancellation data came from BTS's ASQP database, which contains flight-level performance data for non-stop domestic flights by the larger air carriers. Our sample contains 20 airlines. Fifteen of these are major carriers, defined by BTS as having annual revenues in excess of $1 billion.[29] The remaining airlines are national carriers, defined as having annual revenues between $100 million and $1 billion.[30]

To ensure sufficient time series variation for estimating each panel, we omitted route-carrier groups with data spanning less than one year. Furthermore, we excluded observations with either an origin or destination outside the continental U.S. and for flights that arrived more than one hour early or six hours late. We also ignored any route that reported less than eight flights per month. To ensure our sample captured scheduled passenger service exclusively, we used performance data in combination with BTS's T-100 database to identify service type. The T-100 data also included data on aircraft characteristics and load factors, defined as the monthly average ratio of total passengers and seats.

We constructed HHIs, which we used to gauge market competition, based on data from BTS's DB1B database.[31] Our analyses focused on an HHI based on airlines' shares of market revenues.[32] We defined an airline "market" as a directional origin and destination airport-pair. Since less than 5 percent of the passengers in our sample used flights with two or more stops, we only included direct flights and flights requiring one connection as competitors.[33] The market definition is directional so that Washington Dulles (IAD) to Raleigh–Durham International (RDU) is considered to be a different route or airport-pair than RDU to IAD. We chose the directional definition because our measures of service quality often differ for opposite directions on the same route.

We formed our baseline sample by combining the on-time performance data and DB1B-based information.[34] This produced 5,351 directional airport-pairs. The sample size was somewhat reduced after merging with weather data from the National Climatic Data Center because weather information was unavailable for routes where either endpoint airport does not belong to a Metropolitan Statistical Area. The sample was substantially reduced after merging with airport capacity utilization data from the FAA's APM Airport Efficiency System, as that data is only available for 73 of the larger airports.[35] The hourly airport capacity utilization data represents the number of arriving and departing flights an airport completes divided by the maximum number it can safely complete based on the configuration and weather conditions. The merger with this data reduced the final number of directional airport-pairs to 2,530, with 5,481 route-carrier combinations, and 298,389 monthly observations (298,523 for our cancellation model). Even though the number of directional airport-pairs covered in our final sample only accounted for about 50 percent of what we had before the merger with the capacity utilization data, these routes encompassed approximately 71 percent of the total number of flights in the ASQP database.

Model Specification

The basic structure of our model is

$$Y_{ijt} = \alpha X_{jt} + \beta Z_{ijt} + \varepsilon_t + c_{ij} + \mu_{ijt} \tag{1}$$

where i indexes airline, j indexes route, and t indexes time. The dependent variable Y_{ijt} is a service quality variable measuring flight delays or cancellations for airline i on route j at month t. We used two alternative delay definitions. $Delay_{ijt}$ is airline i's monthly average minutes of arrival delays for all flights on route j in month t. $Late\ Flight_{ijt}$ is the monthly percent of airline i's flights on route j that are at least 15 minutes late.[36] $Cancel_{jt}$ is the monthly percent of airline i's flights on route j that are cancelled. We ran three separate estimations for each definition of service quality.

The vector X_{jt} measures airline route or market competition. The vector Z_{ijt} contains other explanatory variables varying by route-carrier and time. ε_t is a vector of yearly and quarterly time effects. In part, ε_t serves to absorb shifts in macroeconomic variables, such as the unemployment rate, as they generally exhibit time series variation but change little across panels. c_{ij} represents the route-carrier heterogeneity. It captures the time invariant factors for each route-carrier combination, such as distance and demographic elements.

In most of our estimations, X_{jt} is comprised of HHI_{jt} , the revenue-based Hirschman-Herfindahl index on route j for month t, so equation (1) becomes

$$Y_{ijt} = \alpha HHI_{jt} + \beta Z_{ijt} + \varepsilon_t + c_{ij} + \mu_{ijt} \tag{2}$$

The endogeneity of HHI in empirical models of airline ticket prices is well documented. We used lagged HHI to instrument for HHI in the current period.

We pursued different approaches to allow for nonlinearities in modeling the length of flight delays versus the percent of late flights and percent of flights cancelled. In the model of delay length, we added a quadratic term, HHI_{jt}^2. In the models of the percent of late and cancelled flights, the dependent variables are bounded by zero and one, so those models are appropriately estimated using a fractional response method.[37] Because this estimation method allows for variable marginal effects, it also readily accommodates any nonlinearities.

The model of delay length was estimated using two-stage least-squares (2SLS).[38] As an alternative means of carrying out the instrumentation, we also used the control function (CF) approach. We used correlated random effects (CRE) to estimate the models of the percent of late and cancelled flights. We followed the implementation in Papke and Wooldridge (2008). We applied the CRE approach to the estimation of the models of the percent of late and cancelled flights in a fractional probit framework. For those models, we corrected for the endogeneity of HHI in the estimation by using the CF approach, as opposed to 2SLS, due to the distinct advantages of applying CF over 2SLS in nonlinear models.[39] In all estimations, we weighted each monthly observation for each route-carrier by the number of flights captured by that monthly average.

Control Variables

We categorized our control variables into weather factors, profitability measures, and route-carrier specific covariates. We used heavy rain and freezing rain to capture the weather events that would be most likely to cause airline delays and cancellations. $Heavy\ Rain\ Origin_{jt}$ is the percent of days in month t at the origin airport of route j with precipitation in excess of the 95th percentile for that airport over the entire sample period. $Freezing\ Rain\ Origin_{jt}$ captures the percent of days in month t with greater than 95th percentile precipitation and a temperature below 32 degrees at the origin airport of route j. $Heavy\ Rain\ Dest_{jt}$ and $Freezing\ Rain\ Dest_{jt}$ similarly capture extreme weather at the destination airport of route j.

We used airline load factors to measure profitability. $Load\ Factor_{ijt}$ is airline i's load factor on route j in month t. Load factor is the total number of passengers divided by the total number of seats. $Depart\ Early_{ijt}$, $Depart\ 6\ am\ to\ 12noon_{ijt}$, $Depart\ 12noon\ to\ 6pm_{ijt}$, $Depart\ 6\ pm\ to\ 12midnight_{ijt}$, represent the monthly percent of route-carrier specific total departures from midnight to 6 am, 6 am to 12 noon, 12 noon to 6 pm, and 6 pm to midnight, respectively. $Depart\ Early_{ijt}$ was our reference group. We introduced these coefficients to capture the effect of cumulative delays, which cause flights scheduled later in a day to be more likely to experience delays and cancellations.

We adapted the congestion measure to the route-carrier level. The airport capacity utilization data reports on the average level of congestion for the airport on an hourly basis. We multiplied this information by the monthly average number of flights for each route-carrier in each hourly interval. This produced a measure allowing two airlines serving the same route to experience different congestion levels at the same airport if one schedules more flights during the morning rush while the other predominantly schedules flights in the afternoon. Accordingly $Congestion\ Origin_{ijt}$ is the sum of the total number of actual flights divided by the maximum allowable number of flights at the origination airport interacted with airline *i*'s hourly departures on route *j*. Similarly $Congestion\ Dest_{ijt}$ captures the route-carrier specific capacity utilization level at the destination airport.

We controlled for the effects of airline hubbing with variables constructed using DB1B data. $Congestion\ Origin_{jt}$ tracks the total number of locations to which there are direct flights from the origin airport of route *j* in the quarter containing month t. Connections $Dest_{jt}$ measures the total number of locations from which there are direct flights to the destination airport of route *j* in the quarter containing month *t*.

We also included aircraft characteristics. We assembled information on aircraft model for each route-carrier combination from T100 data. The seating capacity for each model was identified using data from various aircraft manufacturer Web sites. All aircraft types in our sample were grouped into five categories based on the number of seats. We calculated the monthly average percent of aircraft within each group for each route-carrier combination. $Aircraft\ Group\ 1_{ijt}$ is the monthly percent of all aircraft used by carrier *i* on route *j* comprised of turbo-prop aircraft having up to 70 seats. $Aircraft\ Group\ 2_{ijt}$ to $Aircraft\ Group\ 5_{ijt}$ were generated in similar fashion with higher group numbers representing greater seating capacity.[40]

Other controls included dummy variables for airport expansion and labor actions. Specifically, one set of dummies indicates the completion of airport runway projects in November 2008 at three major airports: Seattle-Tacoma (SEA), Chicago O'Hare (ORD), and Washington Dulles (IAD). For example, $SEA\ Runway\ Origin_{ji}$ is set to one starting November 2008 if the origination airport on route *j* is the Seattle-Tacoma International Airport, and is zero otherwise. $SEA\ Runway\ Dest_{ji}$ similarly indexes the destination airport. The other set of dummies, $Labor\ Strikes_{it}$, indicate periods of labor strikes and slowdowns occurring at different airlines during our sample.[41]

Results

Table B1 displays our regression results, with the standard errors shown in parentheses. The results for the model of arrival delays incorporating the quadratic term clearly indicate that the relationship between the level of competition and minutes of delay is nonlinear. In the FE CF estimation, *v2hat_lag1*, the CF indicator of the need to correct for the endogeneity of the competition measures, is significant. It makes little difference whether we make the correction using 2SLS or the CF.

Table B1. Models of Minutes of Arrival Delays, Percent of Cancelled Flights, and Percent of Late Flights

Dependent Variable	Average Length of Arrival Delays	Average Length of Arrival Delays	Average Percent of Cancelled Flights	Average Percent of Late Flights
	FE 2SLS (IV: 1 Q lagged HHI)	FE CF (IV: 1 Q lagged HHI)	Fprobit CRE CF (IV: 1 Q lagged HHI)	Fprobit CRE CF (IV: 1 Q lagged HHI)
			APE	APE
Revenue Based HHI	11.89***	10.17***	0.00656***	0.00863*
	(3.395)	(2.403)	(0.00113)	(0.00440)
Revenue Based HHI^2	-5.809**	-4.430**		
	(2.554)	(1.751)		
Heavy Rain Origin	20.32***	20.32***	0.0235***	0.213***
	(0.458)	(0.462)	(0.00134)	(0.00491)
Heavy Rain Dest	18.67***	18.67***	0.0226***	0.218***
	(0.449)	(0.453)	(0.00134)	(0.00470)
Freezing Rain Origin	31.68***	31.68***	0.0523***	0.366***
	(0.588)	(0.594)	(0.00131)	(0.00613)
Freezing Rain Dest	18.66***	18.66***	0.0500***	0.197***
	(0.592)	(0.597)	(0.00131)	(0.00603)
Load Factor	19.70***	19.70***	-0.0196***	0.193***
	(0.372)	(0.375)	(0.000937)	(0.00408)
Labor Strikes	7.970***	7.964***	0.00923***	0.107***
	(0.359)	(0.362)	(0.000916)	(0.00443)
Departure 6 am to 12 noon	-3.071***	-3.067***	0.00143	-0.0347***
	(0.511)	(0.516)	(0.00102)	(0.00616)

Dependent Variable	Average Length of Arrival Delays	Average Length of Arrival Delays	Average Percent of Cancelled Flights	Average Percent of Late Flights
	FE 2SLS (IV: 1 Q lagged HHI)	FE CF (IV: 1 Q lagged HHI)	Fprobit CRE CF (IV: 1 Q lagged HHI)	Fprobit CRE CF (IV: 1 Q lagged HHI)
			APE	APE
Departure 12 noon to 6 pm	1.816***	1.823***	0.00503***	0.0269***
	(0.530)	(0.536)	(0.00107)	(0.00637)
Departure 6 pm to 12 midnight	7.032***	7.036***	0.00510***	0.0914***
	(0.558)	(0.564)	(0.00113)	(0.00662)
Connections Origin	0.0454***	0.0449***	-3.61e-05***	0.000429***
	(0.00586)	(0.00591)	(1.26e-05)	(6.31e-05)
Connections Dest	0.00626	0.00586	2.33e-05**	0.000107*
	(0.00548)	(0.00553)	(1.17e-05)	(6.03e-05)
Congestion Origin	10.14***	10.14***	-0.00318***	0.124***
	(0.517)	(0.523)	(0.00116)	(0.00621)
Congestion Dest	12.69***	12.69***	0.00116	0.149***
	(0.588)	(0.593)	(0.00113)	(0.00668)
SEA Runway Origin	-2.479***	-2.479***	-0.00384**	-0.0545***
	(0.519)	(0.520)	(0.00161)	(0.00796)
ORD Runway Origin	-5.153***	-5.158***	-0.00720***	-0.0335***
	(0.428)	(0.433)	(0.000504)	(0.00368)
IAD Runway Origin	-2.603***	-2.597***	-0.00246***	-0.0234***
	(0.595)	(0.607)	(0.000870)	(0.00612)
SEA Runway Dest	-4.415***	-4.414***	-0.00673***	-0.0596***
	(0.744)	(0.746)	(0.00160)	(0.00928)
ORD Runway Dest	-6.840***	-6.845***	-0.00686***	-0.0440***
	(0.403)	(0.408)	(0.000445)	(0.00344)
IAD Runway Dest	-0.316	-0.311	-0.00343***	-0.00114
	(0.572)	(0.579)	(0.000873)	(0.00600)
Aircraft Type Group 3	0.0126	0.0143	-0.00410***	-0.00652
	(0.388)	(0.391)	(0.000504)	(0.00415)
Aircraft Type Group 4	0.176	0.177	-0.00579***	-0.00432
	(0.426)	(0.429)	(0.000605)	(0.00461)
Aircraft Type Group 5	0.672	0.666	-0.00786***	-0.00113
	(0.862)	(0.870)	(0.00102)	(0.00841)
Year 2007	0.0978	0.0976	0.00156***	0.00196*
	(0.0922)	(0.0929)	(0.000199)	(0.00111)

Table B1. (Continued)

Dependent Variable	Average Length of Arrival Delays	Average Length of Arrival Delays	Average Percent of Cancelled Flights	Average Percent of Late Flights
	FE 2SLS (IV: 1 Q lagged HHI)	FE CF (IV: 1 Q lagged HHI)	Fprobit CRE CF (IV: 1 Q lagged HHI)	Fprobit CRE CF (IV: 1 Q lagged HHI)
			APE	APE
Year 2008	-2.478***	-2.481***	-0.00274***	-0.0286***
	(0.0974)	(0.0977)	(0.000230)	(0.00112)
Year 2009	-5.087***	-5.091***	-0.00700***	-0.0515***
	(0.109)	(0.110)	(0.000261)	(0.00121)
Year 2010	-6.088***	-6.092***	-0.00250***	-0.0591***
	(0.142)	(0.144)	(0.000261)	(0.00148)
Year 2011	-5.373***	-5.378***	-0.00104***	-0.0588***
	(0.128)	(0.129)	(0.000263)	(0.00141)
Year 2012	-6.732***	-6.737***	-0.00493***	-0.0757***
	(0.151)	(0.152)	(0.000301)	(0.00171)
Quarter 2	1.170***	1.171***	-0.00297***	0.00120**
	(0.0536)	(0.0542)	(0.000153)	(0.000595)
Quarter 3	0.715***	0.714***	-0.00272***	-0.00776***
	(0.0603)	(0.0607)	(0.000164)	(0.000729)
Quarter 4	-1.018***	-1.019***	-0.00507***	-0.0145***
	(0.0408)	(0.0412)	(0.000150)	(0.000484)
v2hat_lag1		-4.058***	-0.0128***	-0.0194***
		(0.632)	(0.00105)	(0.00489)
Observations	289,248	289,248	288,954	288,810
R-squared	0.216	0.419		
Route Carrier Combinations	5,485			

Notes: *Significant at the 10 percent level. **Significant at the 5 percent level. ***Significant at the 1 percent level.

To further examine the diminishing effects of marginal changes in competition on average delay length, we generated estimates of the marginal effects at different HHI levels. Specifically, we calculated the marginal effects at HHI levels from 0.1 through 0.9, in increments of 0.1, based on the FE CF estimation. Table B2 displays the results. The reported marginal effects of a .1

increase in HHI peak at over 1 minute at HHI=0.1 and decline, as the level of HHI increases, to less than 16 seconds at HHI=.8. They are insignificant at HHI=0.9.

We also found the relationship between competition and airline service quality to be nonlinear when using the flight cancellation rate as the measure of service quality. Table B1 shows the results of estimating the cancellations model using fractional probit with CRE and CF. The fractional probit approach allows us to identify how the average partial effect (APE) changes with the level of HHI. Table B2 presents the APEs evaluated from HHI=0.1 to HHI=0.9 at increments of 0.1. The size of the impact of an increase in competition on the cancellation rate grows at an increasing rate with the level of HHI. Specifically, the APE grows from .055 percent at HHI=0.1 to .073 percent at HHI=0.9. Further, the APE is statistically significant at every HHI level.

The relationship between competition and the percent of late flights is only significant at the 10 percent level in the fractional probit estimation, as Table B1 shows. Table B2 presents the APEs evaluated at different levels of HHI. They do not change much with the level of HHI, but some are significant at the 5 percent level.

Sensitivity Analyses

We tested the sensitivity of our results to the use of different lags of HHI in the instrumentation process and to the use of alternative HHI measures. The other HHI measures included indices of competition: (1) restricted to direct flights connecting airport-pairs; and (2) between all direct and one-stop flights connecting pairs of metropolitan statistical areas (MSA).[42] Lastly, since our panels were unbalanced, we investigated the extent to which attrition and addition in our panel were correlated with idiosyncratic shocks.

Table B3 displays the sensitivity test results derived using the different HHI measures. We found that the relationship between delay length and competition in a linear specification was robust to the instrument being lagged as much as 6 quarters. The relationship between the cancellation rate and competition, is also robust to use of longer lags of the instrumental variable, except in the case of the MSA-pair HHI. In the model of the percent of late flights, the competition measures remain relatively insignificant at all lags of the instrumental variable. Use of the HHI based only on direct flights does not change the qualitative results in any model. However, use of the HHI calculated for MSA-pairs does produce different results: the HHI coefficient is insignificant in the cancellation rate model, and is significant and negative in the model of the percent of late flights.

Wooldridge (2010b) suggests several alternative estimation strategies to address selection bias in the nonlinear CRE framework, including using only those observations for which a balanced panel is available, and performing a separate estimation for each time period. The relationship between competition and cancellation rates was the same or even stronger using these alternative estimation strategies than in our other estimations.

Table B2. Estimated HHI Marginal and Average Partial Effects (APE)

	Length of Delay (Marginal Effects)	Percent of Cancelled Flights (APEs)	Percent of Late Flights (APEs)
	Revenue Based HHI (Direct and One-Stop Flights)	Revenue Based HHI (Direct and One-Stop Flights)	Revenue Based HHI (Direct and One-Stop Flights)
HHI=0.1	10.73***	0.00553***	0.00852**
	(2.906)	(0.000792)	(0.0043)
HHI=0.2	9.569***	0.00573***	0.00855**
	(2.409)	(0.000857)	(0.00432)
HHI=0.3	8.407***	0.00595***	0.00857**
	(1.920)	(0.000926)	(0.00434)
HHI=0.4	7.245***	0.00616***	0.00859**
	(1.450)	(0.000997)	(0.00436)
HHI=0.5	6.083***	0.00639***	0.00861**
	(1.023)	(0.00107)	(0.00439)
HHI=0.6	4.921***	0.00661***	0.00863*
	(0.719)	(0.00115)	(0.00441)
HHI=0.7	3.759***	0.00685***	0.00865*
	(0.719)	(0.00123)	(0.00443)
HHI=0.8	2.597**	0.00709***	0.00867*
	(1.022)	(0.00131)	(0.00445)
HHI=0.9	1.436	0.00734***	0.00869*
	(1.449)	(0.00140)	(0.00447)

Notes: *Significant at the 10 percent level. **Significant at the 5 percent level. ***Significant at the 1 percent level.

Table B3. Sensitivity Test HHI Estimates

	Airport-Pair: Revenue Based HHI (Direct and One-Stop Flights)	Airport-Pair: Revenue Based HHI (Direct Flight Only)	MSA-Pair: Revenue Based HHI (Direct and One-Stop Flights)
	Minutes of Delay Model		
IV: 1 Quarter Lag	4.648***	3.693***	4.457***
	(0.661)	(0.517)	(0.850)
IV: 2 Quarter Lag	5.767***	5.142***	5.590***
	(0.931)	(0.741)	(1.165)
IV: 3 Quarter Lag	4.206***	3.966***	3.006**
	(1.264)	(1.011)	(1.453)
IV: 4 Quarter Lag	4.881***	5.362***	2.040
	(1.611)	(1.307)	(1.656)
IV: 5 Quarter Lag	5.901**	6.992***	2.357
	(2.617)	(2.137)	(2.481)
IV: 6 Quarter Lag	13.89***	14.70***	6.842*
	(4.815)	(4.153)	(3.742)
Percent of Cancelled Flight Model			
IV: 1 Quarter Lag	0.00656***	0.00272***	0.000876
	(0.00113)	(0.000932)	(0.00108)
IV: 2 Quarter Lag	0.00661***	0.00282***	0.000812
	(0.00117)	(0.000964)	(0.00110)
IV: 3 Quarter Lag	0.00650***	0.00281***	0.000593
	(0.00119)	(0.000992)	(0.00112)
IV: 4 Quarter Lag	0.00639***	0.00275***	0.000656
	(0.00121)	(0.00101)	(0.00114)
IV: 5 Quarter Lag	0.00662***	0.00333***	0.00113
	(0.00122)	(0.00102)	(0.00118)
IV: 6 Quarter Lag	0.00646***	0.00341***	0.00128
	(0.00121)	(0.00101)	(0.00118)
Percent of Late Flight Model			
IV: 1 Quarter Lag	0.00863*	0.00256	-0.0198***
	(0.00440)	(0.00384)	(0.00494)
IV: 2 Quarter Lag	0.00788*	0.00223	-0.0204***
	(0.00455)	(0.00399)	(0.00509)
IV: 3 Quarter Lag	0.00474	-0.000623	-0.0223***
	(0.00466)	(0.00408)	(0.00519)

Table B3. (Continued)

	Airport-Pair: Revenue Based HHI (Direct and One-Stop Flights)	Airport-Pair: Revenue Based HHI (Direct Flight Only)	MSA-Pair: Revenue Based HHI (Direct and One-Stop Flights)
	Minutes of Delay Model		
IV: 4 Quarter Lag	0.00396	-0.000498	-0.0236***
	(0.00472)	(0.00415)	(0.00526)
IV: 5 Quarter Lag	0.00392	-0.000435	-0.0244***
	(0.00481)	(0.00424)	(0.00540)
IV: 6 Quarter Lag	0.00667	0.00207	-0.0228***
	(0.00492)	(0.00435)	(0.00559

Notes: *Significant at the 10 percent level. **Significant at the .5 percent level. ***Significant at the 1 percent level.

EXHIBIT C. MAJOR CONTRIBUTORS TO THIS REPORT

Name	Title
Betty Krier	Supervisory Economist/Program Director
Chia-Mei Liu	Senior Economist (Lead)
Kang Hua Cao	Senior Economist
Brian McNamara	Senior Economist
Jerrod Sharpe	Senior Economist
Tom Denomme	Audit Expert
Susan Neill	Writer/Editor
Joshua Ingber	Economist Intern

REFERENCES

Papke, L. E. & Wooldridge. J. M. (2008). Panel Data Methods for Fractional Response Variables with an Application to Test Pass Rates, *Journal of Econometrics*, *145*, 121-33.

Wooldridge, J. M. (2010a). *Econometric Analysis of Cross Section and Panel Data*, Second Edition.

Wooldridge, J. M. (2010b). Correlated Random Effects Models with Unbalanced Panels, working paper.

End Notes

[1] The Economics Group, which conducts analyses across all modes and produced this audit, is situated in the Surface Transportation Group as of April 1, 2014.

[2] The figures in this paragraph are derived using the Bureau of Transportation Statistics On-time Performance database. Coverage limitations of the available data on airline delays and cancellations are discussed in *More Comprehensive Data Are Needed to Better Understand the Nation's Flight Delays and Their Causes* (OIG Report No. AV-2014-016), December 18, 2013. OIG reports are available on our Web site: http://www.oig.dot.gov.

[3] The Subcommittee on Antitrust, Competition Policy, and Consumer Rights, Senate Committee on the Judiciary, and the Ranking Member of Subcommittee on Aviation, House Committee on Transportation and Infrastructure requested that the General Accountability Office investigate airline competition issues.

[4] Pub. L. No. 112-95 §406 (2012).

[5] This excludes Alaska, Hawaii and U.S. Territories.

[6] This includes 15 major carriers and 5 national carriers. Major carriers have annual revenues over $1 billion. National carriers have annual revenues between $100 million to $1 billion.

[7] When referenced in this manner, airlines are assumed to be of equal size.

[8] The effects of reduced competition on the frequency of late flights were the same at all levels of competition and only minimally statistically significant overall.

[9] A relationship or effect is statistically significant if it is unlikely to have occurred through random chance. The less likely it is that the relationship or effect occurred though random chance, the more statistically significant is the relationship or effect. For further detail on our testing for statistical significance, see exhibit B.

[10] Exhibit B details our sample construction process. It was primarily determined by the availability of data on the factors to be included in our analysis, in particular airport congestion and weather.

[11] Our control variables included measures of weather conditions, profitability, labor actions, congestion, and runway expansions (see exhibits A and B).

[12] We measured the length of delay considering both positive minutes of delay as well as negative minutes of delay to incorporate all information on timeliness of all flights in our estimation.

[13] We considered a flight late if it arrived 15 minutes or more after the scheduled arrival time.

[14] Direct flight refers to non-stop flights and flights with one stop but no change of aircraft. We use this definition because the data in Bureau of Transportation Statistics' Data and Airline Origin and Destination survey (DB1B) does not support distinguishing between non-stop flights and flights with one stop but no change of plane. Most passengers in DB1B are on direct flights.

[15] Less than 5 percent of the passengers in our sample had trips with two or more stops.

[16] Rounding error prevents these percentages from adding up to 100.

[17] It was significant at the 1 percent level.

[18] Figures 2, 4, 6, 7 and 8 depict impacts estimated using our econometric models.

[19] It was only significant at the 10 percent level.

[20] It was significant at the 1 percent level.

[21] These small percentages translate into large numbers of flights. In our sample, roughly 1.6 percent of flights were cancelled, which translated into more than 70,000 cancelled flights annually on average.

[22] All the results reported in this section derive from our statistical analysis.

[23] These HHI change estimates assume all airlines split the market equally.

[24] These were: ATA, AirTran, Alaska, American, American Eagle, Comair, Continental, Delta, Frontier, JetBlue, Northwest, SkyWest, Southwest, US Airways, and United.

[25] These were: Atlantic Southeast, ExpressJet, Mesa, Pinnacle, and Virgin America.

[26] All airlines operating any aircraft having over 60 seats are required to report.

[27] The capacity utilization data was based on FAA's "called rates," which are the maximum hourly number of arriving and departing flights an airport can safely handle as determined by air traffic control given existing operational conditions, such as wind direction and weather. See Exhibit B for further information.

[28] *More Comprehensive Data Are Needed To Better Understand the Nation's Flight Delays and Their Causes*, OIG Report Number AV-2014-016,,December 18, 2013, discusses the coverage limitations of this data.

[29] They are: ATA, AirTran, Alaska, America West, American, American Eagle, Comair, Continental, Delta, Frontier, JetBlue, Northwest, SkyWest, Southwest, US Airways, and United.

[30] They are: Atlantic Southeast, ExpressJet, Mesa, Pinnacle, and Virgin America.

[31] Data Base Products was the provider of our DB1B data. They identify and eliminate a number of data errors, and consolidate the data into a more manageable format.

[32] We also constructed HHIs based on shares of market passengers, shares of non-stop service revenues, and shares of market revenues from all flights connecting metropolitan statistical areas rather than airport-pairs. We used these additional HHIs to conduct sensitivity analyses.

[33] A direct flight means a non-stop flight, although technically, it also includes a flight with one stop but no change of aircraft. This definition arises because the data in DB1B does not support distinguishing between a non-stop flight versus a flight with one stop but no change of plane. Most passengers in DB1B are on direct flights.

[34] The merging process presented a challenge as the Aviation On-Time Performance Data is associated with the operating carrier, while each observation in the DB1B data is tied to a combination of an operating carrier and a marketing carrier. Further, we base the HHI calculation on the marketing carriers. Since about 50 percent of the observations have an operating carrier that is different from the marketing carrier, we merged these two data sets by operating carrier using the following rules: (1) for records that link multiple operating carriers to the same marketing carrier, we simply merged by operating carrier. (2) For records that link multiple marketing carriers to the same operating carrier, we identified the dominant marketing carrier, which for 99.5 percent of these observations was the one with equal to or greater than 50 percent O&D passenger share and performed the merger by eliminating duplicate records with the same operating carrier.

[35] FAA collects data on a total of 77 airports, but only 73 airports are within the lower 48 states. Merging with the data on cancellations and on delays further reduced our coverage to 70 airports. The airport capacity data is not publicly available. We gained access through FAA.

[36] BTS designates a flight late if it arrives at least 15 minutes past schedule.

[37] The application of panel data methods to fractional response models is explained in detail by Papke and Wooldridge (2008).

[38] We predicted the values of the linear and quadratic forms of HHI separately in the first stage.

[39] These advantages are discussed in Wooldridge (2010a), pp. 126-128 and 589.

[40] Group 2 includes regional jets with up to 70 seats. Group 3 contains regional jets with 70 to 100 seats. Group 4 is made up of narrow body planes having more than 100 seats. Group 5 represents all wide body aircraft.

[41] We collected information on airline labor actions from sources such as the Wall Street Journal, the Chicago Tribune, the Bureau of Labor Statistics, CNN, USA Today, NBC news, TribLive, and Highbeam. Four events were identified during our sample, affecting: (1) Northwest Airlines from October to November 2005; (2) Northwest Airlines in November 2006; (3) US Airways in April 2006; and (4) American Airlines from September to October 2012.

[42] Another set of specifications we tried used HHIs based on the number of passengers in each market. The results differed little from those produced using revenue--based indices, so we only report on the revenue-based HHI estimations.

INDEX

A

access, 3, 16, 35, 37, 38, 41, 44, 45, 46, 82, 112
accessibility, 99
accountability, 88
acquisitions, 7, 10, 17, 54, 66, 69, 70, 71, 72, 73, 84, 86
adverse effects, vii, 1, 44
advocacy, viii, 2, 5, 35, 37, 39, 40, 41, 42, 44, 45, 50, 51
agencies, 35, 40, 47, 50, 51, 54, 85
air carriers, 100
airfares, vii, 1, 3, 4, 13, 15, 28, 30, 57, 63
airline competition, vii, viii, 1, 2, 3, 4, 5, 36, 38, 46, 50, 57, 63, 92, 93, 97, 99, 111
airline industry, vii, viii, 1, 3, 5, 7, 10, 11, 12, 35, 40, 41, 43, 45, 46, 47, 50, 54, 55, 59, 61, 62, 63, 64, 66, 67, 84, 85, 90
airline mergers, vii, viii, 1, 2, 4, 9, 10, 19, 23, 26, 54, 62, 64, 69, 70, 71, 72, 73
airline revenues, 14
airline service quality, vii, viii, 88, 89, 90, 96, 99, 107
airport hubs, 77
airports, 3, 5, 9, 17, 27, 28, 29, 31-34, 36-38, 41, 44, 47, 50, 53, 56-58, 60, 68, 71, 73, 74, 77, 82, 83, 90, 98, 100, 103, 112
Alaska, 20, 46, 51, 53, 75, 111, 112
Aloha, 84
American Society of Travel Agents, 51
analytical framework, 10, 62, 70
antitrust, 10, 42, 45, 54, 62, 63, 66, 70, 71, 83, 84, 86
APA, 76
Asia, 43
assessment, 10
assets, 7, 53, 54, 55, 70, 71, 73, 75, 84
audit, 6, 51, 64, 87, 88, 97, 98, 111
authority(s), 5, 35, 44, 50, 51, 54, 64, 66, 70, 71, 83, 84, 85
aviation industry, 5, 47
avoidance, 59

B

baggage, 2, 6, 16, 28, 31, 40, 55, 59
balance sheet, 73
bankruptcy(s), 4, 7, 12, 17, 53, 55, 63, 64, 66, 67, 68, 70, 71, 74, 85
bargaining, 7
barriers, 3, 10, 36, 37, 39, 43, 44, 72, 73, 83
barriers to entry, 10, 37, 44, 73
base, 30, 41, 58, 112
BBB, 12, 55
benefits, 10, 43, 44, 45, 54, 55, 59, 62, 63, 70, 71, 72, 73, 84, 85
bias, 108
bonds, 58
bonuses, 12
Bureau of Labor Statistics, 112
business model, 63

business strategy, 26
business travelers, 9, 37

C

cancellation rates, viii, ix, 88, 89, 93, 94, 95, 97, 108
Caribbean, 6
cash, 2, 12, 53
certificate, 85
certification, 10
Chad, 85
challenges, vii, viii, 2, 3, 4, 5, 35, 38, 42, 43, 45, 46, 50, 74, 86
Chicago, 26, 27, 29, 33, 54, 56, 58, 74, 82, 86, 103, 112
China, 43
city(s), 3, 5, 9, 20, 21, 22, 24, 26, 31, 47, 48, 49, 52, 53, 56, 60, 77, 83, 86
CNN, 112
collective bargaining, 85
commercial, 32, 38, 48, 53, 56, 58, 86
commodity, 35
community(s), 6, 25, 32, 33, 34, 41, 46, 63, 64, 84, 88
compensation, 18
competition policy, 4
competitive advantage, 45
competitive conditions, 47, 56
competitive markets, 95, 97
competitiveness, 90
competitors, 2, 10, 19, 20, 21, 22, 23, 24, 25, 26, 29, 35, 37, 42, 47, 48, 54, 56, 57, 62, 70, 77, 83, 100
computer, 7, 26, 73, 74
computer systems, 7, 73
configuration, 100
Congress, vii, 1, 4, 44, 58
congressional hearings, 88
connectivity, 33, 34, 72, 86
consent, 54, 71, 85
consolidation, vii, 1, 3, 4, 7, 9, 23, 24, 25, 29, 31, 36, 37, 41, 44, 73, 88
construction, 98, 99, 111
consumer advocates, 41
consumer choice, 10
consumer loyalty, 35
consumer protection, 44
consumers, vii, viii, 1, 2, 3, 4, 5, 9, 25, 28, 30, 31, 34, 35, 36, 39, 40, 41, 42, 45, 46, 50, 59, 62, 63, 66, 71, 72, 83
Continental, viii, 7, 17, 25, 26, 33, 46, 53, 54, 61, 63, 66, 68, 74, 77, 81, 84, 86, 88, 111, 112
Continental Airlines, viii, 25, 33, 46, 53, 54, 61, 63, 84
cooperation, 97
cooperative agreements, 43
cost, 2, 4, 6, 7, 10-15, 17-20, 24, 25, 27, 29, 30, 34, 35, 37-41, 44, 45, 46, 47, 53, 55, 56, 57, 58, 63, 68, 73, 77, 84, 86
cost saving, 45, 73
court approval, 70, 85
credit rating, 12, 35, 47, 51
creditors, 53, 66, 85
customer loyalty, 35
customers, 30

D

data collection, 46, 47, 49
data set, 48, 112
database, 49, 98, 99, 100, 101, 111
DCA, 75, 82
defined benefit pension, 66
Delta, viii, 4, 7, 12, 16, 17, 25, 27, 33, 39, 46, 51, 53, 59, 61, 63, 64, 66, 68, 75, 77, 82, 84, 88, 111, 112
Delta Air Lines, viii, 4, 12, 17, 25, 27, 46, 51, 53, 61, 63
Department of Justice, 3, 5, 50, 62, 63, 69, 85, 86
Department of Transportation, v, 3, 5, 46, 50, 53, 58, 59, 62, 63, 85, 87, 97
dependent variable, 99, 101, 102
deregulation, 4, 6, 7, 53, 63, 66, 67
disclosure, 36, 40
disposition, 71
distribution, 31, 40, 54, 90
divestiture, 85

DOJ, viii, 2, 3, 5, 9, 10, 23, 26, 38, 41, 45, 50, 54, 57, 61, 62, 63, 64, 66, 68, 69, 70, 71, 72, 74, 76, 77, 83, 84, 85, 86
domestic airlines, vii, 1, 7, 9, 28, 42
domestic markets, 19, 39, 42
dominance, 72
draft, viii, 2, 38, 45, 97

E

earnings, 7, 55
economic downturn, 31
economics, 99
economies of scale, 33
employees, 6, 12, 44, 63, 66, 74, 84
employment, 7, 74
endogeneity, 101, 102, 104
enforcement, 44, 54, 84
environment, 43, 59
epidemic, 7
equity, 54, 72
Europe, 83
evidence, 6, 23, 51, 64, 92, 97
exercise, 9, 10
expertise, viii, 2, 50
exposure, 55
external shocks, 7

F

FAA, 3, 38, 44, 58, 71, 82, 86, 88, 97, 98, 99, 100, 112
fear, 37
federal agency, 54
federal authorities, viii, 62, 64
federal government, vii, viii, 2, 3, 5, 36, 38, 43, 44, 45, 46, 50, 53, 66, 67, 84
federal regulations, 36
filters, 47
financial, vii, viii, 1, 2, 4, 5, 7, 11, 12, 13, 17, 35, 37, 42, 43, 46, 51, 54, 55, 62, 63, 64, 66, 67, 70, 71, 72, 73, 85
financial condition, viii, 46, 62, 64
financial crisis, 4, 7
financial data, viii, 2, 5, 11, 62, 64
financial distress, 7
financial documents,, viii, 62
financial performance, 7, 11, 17, 46
financial resources, 71
financial stability, 66
fixed costs, 7
flexibility, 55
flight(s), viii, ix, 3, 6, 7, 9, 14, 18, 26, 28-32, 34, 35, 40, 41, 42, 44, 53, 57, 83, 88-93, 95, 97-103, 107, 108, 111, 112
flight delays, viii, 34, 57, 88, 89, 90, 91, 97, 98, 99, 101
force, 44
Ford, 58
formula, 58
freezing, 99, 102
fuel prices, 4, 7, 12, 14, 18, 31, 35, 55, 67, 68
funds, 58

G

GAO, vii, viii, 1, 2, 11, 13, 15, 16, 19, 21, 22, 24, 32, 33, 36, 46, 49-62, 67, 69, 80, 81, 84, 85, 86
global competition, 45
grants, 58
graph, 93
grouping, 60
growth, 2, 7, 13, 14, 16, 18, 20, 29, 37, 42, 63, 67, 68
guidelines, 64

H

Hawaii, 20, 111
health, vii, 1, 5, 7, 11, 12, 13, 43, 46, 63
hedging, 55, 56
heterogeneity, 101
host, 83
House, 4, 111
House Committee on Transportation and Infrastructure, 111

House of Representatives, 4
hub, 5, 6, 17, 26, 27, 28, 29, 31, 32, 33, 34, 38, 46, 50, 53, 57, 77, 83, 84
hypothesis, 57

I

IAM, 76
idiosyncratic, 107
immunity, 42, 45, 83
income, 55, 84
increased competition, 63
incumbents, 38
individuals, 5
industry(s), vii, viii, 1, 2, 4, 5, 6, 7, 9, 10, 11, 12, 13, 14, 16, 18, 35, 37, 38, 39, 40, 41, 42, 43, 44, 45, 46, 50, 51, 53, 54, 56, 59, 60, 63, 64, 66, 67, 68, 69, 70, 84, 88
industry consolidation, viii, 43, 44, 88
inflation, 28, 58
information technology, 74
infrastructure, 34, 37, 58
integration, 74
interface, 46
Internal Revenue Service, 44
international competition, 36, 43
investment, 12, 55, 84
issues, viii, 2, 6, 38, 43, 50, 53, 63, 64, 88, 111

L

labor force, 26, 62
landings, 36, 58
Latin America, 6
laws, 42, 45, 54, 66, 71, 85
lead, 10, 28, 42, 54
leisure, 6, 34, 57
light, 41
liquidity, 12
loan guarantees, 67, 84
long-term debt, 12
lower prices, 84
loyalty, 30, 35, 36, 39, 44, 72
Luo, 50

M

magnitude, viii, 62, 63
majority, 2, 27, 37, 43, 58, 63
management, 66
market concentration, 10, 23, 47, 54
market share, 2, 7, 10, 14, 23, 25, 27, 47, 48, 53, 54, 56, 72, 77, 81, 83, 86, 98
market structure, 5, 10, 20, 23, 46, 47
marketing, 10, 35, 42, 53, 83, 86, 112
memorandums of understanding, 74
merger agreement, viii, 61
mergers, viii, 2, 7, 9, 17, 19, 20, 25, 31, 42, 43, 45, 54, 61, 62, 63, 64, 66, 67, 68, 72, 73, 84, 85, 86, 88
methodology, 6, 60, 88, 99
metropolitan areas, 20, 32
Miami, 26, 58, 74, 77, 82
Middle East, 43
model specification, 99
models, 46, 88, 90, 99, 101, 102, 111, 112
monopoly, 21, 56, 71, 90
Montana, 21, 25
multiple factors, 27

N

National Research Council, 59
negative effects, viii, 62, 63
negotiating, 17
net profit margin, 13
North America, 51
Northwest Airlines, viii, 25, 33, 34, 46, 53, 59, 61, 63, 112

O

obstacles, 38, 39
Office of Management and Budget, 38
officials, viii, 2, 5, 37, 38, 40, 46, 47, 49, 50, 64, 83
on-time performance, viii, 88, 98, 100

operating costs, 7, 18, 39, 43, 68, 73
operating revenues, 13, 16, 30, 55, 63, 74
operations, 6, 7, 17, 26, 33, 38, 42, 53, 55, 58, 64, 71, 72, 73, 75, 84
opportunities, 32, 59
optimization, 72
organizational culture, 74
overlap, 33, 62, 77
oversight, 4, 45
ownership, 43, 59, 72

P

Pacific, 66
participants, 42, 55, 83
passenger airline, vii, viii, 1, 2, 4, 6, 11, 14, 37, 46, 54, 61, 62, 63, 74, 86
passenger itinerary, viii, 2, 29
passenger travel, 83
pension plans, 55, 66, 84
percentile, 102
Persian Gulf, 45
Philadelphia, 26, 75, 77, 82, 83
policy, 42, 45, 68
potential benefits, viii, 62, 63
precipitation, 102
president, 99
principles, 28
procurement, 73
profit, 12
profitability, 2, 12, 13, 14, 99, 102, 111
protection, 7, 45, 63, 70, 71, 85
public interest, 41, 59, 71

Q

quality control, 5, 46, 47, 49
query, 46

R

real terms, 3, 28
recession, 2, 4, 7, 11, 12, 13, 14, 18, 28, 29, 39, 42, 67
recommendations, 47
recovery, 2, 11, 14
Reform, 58, 88, 98
regression, 104
regulations, 42, 58, 71
reliability, 5, 46, 47, 49, 64
relief, 71
requirements, 38, 55, 58, 84
researchers, 50
reserves, 2, 12
resolution, 41
response, 28, 42, 102, 112
restrictions, 3, 43, 59
restructuring, 17, 68, 73, 85
revenue, 2, 3, 6, 14, 15, 16, 30, 31, 44, 53, 55, 57, 72, 73, 75, 90, 101, 112
rewards, 39
rights, 4, 37, 59, 68
risk, 12, 54, 55
routes, 7, 10, 15, 20, 29, 34, 39, 42, 47, 56, 60, 62, 66, 71, 72, 73, 76, 83, 90, 100
rules, 43, 44, 58, 112

S

safety, 54, 59, 70, 71
SARS, 7
savings, 62, 73
schedule information, viii, 62
scope, viii, 6, 25, 61, 70, 88, 99
SEA, 103, 105
security(s), 54, 59, 70, 84
Senate, 4, 61, 111
Senate Committee on the Judiciary, 111
sensitivity, 99, 107, 112
September 11, 4, 67
service quality, vii, viii, 88, 89, 90, 96, 99, 100, 101, 107
services, 2, 3, 4, 16, 30, 35, 47, 51, 55, 58, 59, 66
shareholders, 12, 54, 72
shock, 67
signs, 45
small communities, 31, 34
small firms, 23

South America, 43
specifications, 112
stakeholders, vii, viii, 2, 3, 5, 35, 37, 38, 39, 40, 41, 42, 43, 44, 45, 46, 47, 50
standard error, 104
state(s), vii, 1, 3, 9, 26, 44, 45, 58, 59, 112
statistics, 74
statutory authority, 42, 54
stock, 12, 54, 63, 72
structure, vii, 2, 3, 5, 10, 19, 26, 35, 43, 46, 49, 101
substitutes, 90
Sun, 84, 86
Supreme Court, 45

T

taxes, 15, 28, 40, 45, 58
technical comments, viii, 2, 45
technology, 35, 73, 74
temperature, 102
terrorist attack, 7, 67
testing, 64, 111
time series, 98, 100, 101
tracks, 103
trade, 5, 35, 39, 42, 43, 45, 47, 50, 51, 66, 85
transparency, 3, 36, 44
transport, 16, 18, 56
transportation, 5, 9, 18, 34, 42, 44, 48, 53, 59, 71, 85

U

U.S. airline industry, vii, viii, 2, 5, 13, 14, 16, 17, 25, 30, 46, 88
unemployment rate, 101
unions, 17, 74
unit cost, 18, 46, 55
United, v, viii, 1, 4, 7, 16, 17, 25, 26, 33, 39, 46, 49, 53, 54, 55, 57, 58, 59, 61, 62, 63, 64, 66, 68, 71, 74, 75, 77, 81, 82, 83, 84, 85, 86, 88, 111, 112
United Airlines, viii, 4, 25, 46, 53, 61, 63, 71, 84
United States, v, viii, 1, 4, 7, 49, 57, 58, 59, 61, 63, 66, 71, 83, 85
United-Continental merger, 64
universe, 54
US Airways, v, viii, 2, 4, 7, 17, 19, 26, 34, 38, 41, 46, 53, 54, 55, 58, 59, 61, 62, 63, 64, 66, 68, 71, 72, 73, 74, 75, 76, 77, 79, 81, 82, 83, 84, 85, 86, 88, 111, 112
USA, 112

V

variables, 99, 101, 102, 103, 111
variations, 88
vector, 101
veto, 37, 58
volatility, 7, 11, 55
voting, 54, 66, 70, 84
vulnerability, 54

W

Washington, 3, 9, 20, 38, 44, 53-55, 57, 58, 59, 68, 75, 82, 83, 84, 85, 86, 100, 103
websites, 35
Wi-Fi, 16, 30, 35, 41
windows, 99
workers, 55, 84
workforce, 18, 74
worldwide, 59, 83

X

XML, 3, 40

Y

yield, 29, 62